THE WAY OF
HERMES

THE WAY OF HERMES

New Translations of *The Corpus Hermeticum* and
The Definitions of Hermes Trismegistus to Asclepius

CLEMENT SALAMAN, DORINE VAN OYEN,
WILLIAM D. WHARTON, JEAN-PIERRE MAHÉ

Inner Traditions
Rochester, Vermont

Inner Traditions International
One Park Street
Rochester, Vermont 05767
www.InnerTraditions.com

First U.S. edition published in 2000 by Inner Traditions International
First U.S. paperback edition published in 2004

Originally published in 1999 by Gerald Duckworth & Co. Ltd., London

THE LIBRARY OF CONGRESS HAS CATALOGED THE HARDCOVER EDITION AS FOLLOWS:
Corpus Hermeticum. English
     The way of Hermes : translations of The Corpus Hermeticum and
The definitions of Hermes Trismegistus to Asclepius / [translated by] Clement
Salaman ... [et al.].–1st U.S. ed.
          p. cm.
     Originally published: London : G. Duckworth & Co., 1999.
     Includes bibliographical references and index.
     ISBN 0-89281-817-4 (hardcover)
        1. Hermetism. I. Hermes, Trismegistus. Definitions of Hermes Trismegistus
to Asclepius. II. Salaman, Clement. III. Title.

BF1600 .C6713 2000
135'.45—dc21

                                          99-086338

ISBN of paperback edition: ISBN 978-0-89281-186-1

Printed and bound in the United States

12 11

This book was typeset in Garamond BE Regular

Contents

Plates between pages 48 and 49

That Light whose smile kindles the universe,
That Beauty in which all things work and move,
That Benediction which the eclipsing Curse
Of birth can quench not, that sustaining Love
Which, through the web of being blindly wove
By man and beast and earth and air and sea,
Burns bright or dim, as each are mirrors of
The fire for which all thirst, now beams on me,
Consuming the last clouds of cold mortality.

Shelley, *Adonais*

The Corpus Hermeticum

translated by

Clement Salaman
Dorine van Oyen
William D. Wharton

Preface

In the year 1460 a monk brought a Greek manuscript to Florence. The monk, Leonardo of Pistoia, was one of the agents that the city's ruler, Cosimo de' Medici, had sent to scour Europe's monasteries for forgotten writings of the ancients, and what he now brought his patron was a codex containing fourteen treatises attributed to Hermes Trismegistus, an ancient Egyptian sage. This work's arrival caused a great stir, because Hermes, identified with the Ibis god Thoth, was held to be older than Plato and Moses and the underlying inspiration of all philosophy and religion that followed him. Cosimo immediately instructed his scholar Marsilio Ficino to suspend his project of translating the complete dialogues of the divine Plato so that he might undertake a translation of this even more significant work.

This manuscript contained the nucleus of the *Corpus Hermeticum*, also falsely called *Pimander*, after the first treatise, *Poimandres*. Along with some astrological and alchemical works, also named after Hermes, these tracts became the fundamental writings of the Renaissance, together called Hermeticism, whereas the doctrine of the *Corpus Hermeticum* is called Hermetism. The texts of the *Corpus* are preserved in Greek, and appear to have been produced between the first and third centuries AD in Alexandria, Egypt.

In 1614 the Swiss Calvinist from Geneva, Casaubon, proved that the *Corpus Hermeticum* was not as old as it pretended to be but should be dated after the beginning of the Christian era. After this Hermetic writings lost their general fascination but lived on in secret societies such as the Freemasons and the Rosicrucians. The discovery of Hermetic writings in one of the thirteen codices found near Nag Hammadi in Egypt in 1945 changed this situation completely. They contained a better version in Coptic of parts of the Hermetic *Asclepius*, preserved in Latin among the works of Apuleius, and moreover, the integral text of an unknown writing called 'On the Ogdoad and Ennead'. This work shows without any doubt that the Hermetic believer was initiated into several grades before transcending the sphere of the seven planets and the heaven of the fixed stars (the Ogdoad). Then he would behold the God beyond and experience Himself. It is now completely certain that there existed before and after the beginning of the Christian era in Alexandria a secret society, akin to a Masonic lodge. The members of this group called themselves 'brethren,' were initiated through a baptism of the Spirit, greeted each other with a sacred kiss, celebrated a sacred meal and read the Hermetic writings as edifying treatises for their spiritual progress.

Moreover, the criticisms of Casaubon lost much of their force. For even if the *Corpus Hermeticum* was written down rather late, its concepts could easily be very old and Egyptian. And in fact the basic principles of emanation, of the world as an overflow from God, and of man as a ray of sunlight ('All is one, all is from the One') are typically ancient Egyptian.

Nor should the influence of esoteric Judaism be neglected. There existed at that time in Alexandria and Palestine a 'Throne Mysticism', in which the initiated rose through the seven palaces of Heaven to behold the 'Kabod', the luminous glory of God in the shape of a Man. This mysticism was inspired by the vision of *Ezekiel 1*, a throne carried by four living beings, above which was a figure like the appearance of a Man, still today the foundation of all Jewish mysticism about Adam Qadmon, archetypal Man. In the *Poimandres* God brings forth the Anthropos, Man, who descends to create and falls into matter. That echoes the main theme of esoteric Judaism.

In the century before Christ the influential Stoic philosopher Posidonius taught that the Cosmos was dominated by the 'sympathy of all things' (stars and events on earth), that God was a Spirit, which pervaded the All, and that man was consubstantial with God, because he had a Spirit. At the same time a certain Eudorus, a Platonist, was teaching in Alexandria, stressing the religious elements, like reincarnation, in Plato and trying to reconcile Plato with Aristotle. The Hermetists followed these figures in using philosophic language to express fundamentally religious teachings.

Thus, Hermetic Studies have been completely renewed. Therefore the time has come for a new translation, which sees the Greek text in the light of the new discoveries and finds an adequate wording in a modern idiom not tainted by the prejudices of old-fashioned rationalism.

Gilles Quispel
Professor Emeritus, Utrecht and Harvard

Acknowledgments

We would like to thank all those who have assisted in the preparation of this edition. Professor Gilles Quispel kindly supported our efforts and contributed the preface. Professor Jean-Pierre Mahé was also most generous in agreeing to publish his translation of the *Definitions* with an introduction in this volume. The following provided reliable and enthusiastic help in the translation: Martin Block, Keith Herndon, Kenneth Larsen, Kathleen Lehmann, Edith Murphy, John Murphy and Danae Wharton. Meta Cushing was of great assistance in preparing notes and the text for publication. Others have given the introductory sections and afterword thoughtful scrutiny, and to them we are most grateful.

We also thank all those who, before publication, read or heard the translation, and who, by their enthusiasm, have encouraged us in our work. Above all, we are indebted to the late Leon MacLaren, who initiated and inspired this translation, which we now dedicate to him.

Translators' Foreword

The heart of the Hermetic teaching contained in this book is the realisation that the individual is fundamentally no different from the Supreme. This realisation is *gnosis,* a single, immediate event, characterised as a second birth. This teaching outlines the spiritual path that prepares the way for this *gnosis,* which is not achieved by any effort of the ordinary mind. The words of the teacher work independently of the disciple's thinking. The point of these treatises is not to argue the truth of their propositions; their meaning is the change they effect in the hearts of their readers or listeners in awakening them to the truth.

We feel that there is a need for a new translation whose language reflects the inspirational intent of these writings. It is not enough to provide a literal translation, however accurate, for unless it reproduces something of the music and poetry of the original, it will not touch the same emotional chord. Our aim is to create an English version whose clarity and cadence evoke the transforming connection with the sacred that drew the original listeners together.

A further reason why we have embarked on a new translation is because we feel that the manuscript tradition could and should be followed far more closely, where it can be, without damage to the sense or logic of the Greek. At times this approach seems to open up the text in fresh and interesting ways. We have primarily consulted the fourteenth-century manuscript Laurentianus 71.33 and the sixteenth-century Bodleianus 3037, as well as the sixteenth-century edition of Adrien Turnebus, closely related to Vindobonensis phil.102. We have also relied on the critical edition of A.D. Nock and A.J. Festugière. There are some places where it has not been possible to follow the manuscripts, because they simply do not make sense. For those passages we have followed Nock's Greek text. For simplicity's sake we have included textual notes only on those occasions when we have departed from Nock's text. We have also kept explanatory notes to a minimum to allow the translation to speak for itself.

As we prepared our translation we spoke with Jean-Pierre Mahé of the Sorbonne about his work on the *Definitions of Hermes Trismegistus*, a Greek manuscript which was found in Oxford's Bodleian Library and brought to light by J. Paramelle in 1991 (see Mahé, 'Extraits Hermétiques', p. 109). Our conversation led to Mahé's most generous agreement to include his translation of that work, along with his introduction, in this edition. We feel fortunate to be able to present his valuable insights into the nature and composition of this teaching, as well as the *Definitions* – aphorisms which, as he argues, formed the basis of the *Corpus* and other Hermetic writings.

Recent arguments for greater Egyptian influence on the *Corpus* (see Professor Quispel's Preface and our Afterword) disposed us to approach our task with particular care. The temptation was to abide by the traditional renderings of the Greek philosophical vocabulary, but such a decision would have given the translation a cast that was at times excessively Platonic, Aristotelian or Stoic. For example, we generally preferred 'nature' or 'essence' to the Aristotelian 'substance' for *ousia*. We usually left *Nous* untranslated, feeling that 'intellect' or 'mind' were inadequate for the pure, conscious light of Book 1.4 or the creative intelligence of the cosmos of Books 1 and 10. As with most terms, however, we were by no means inflexible in our decisions: when the context suggested discursive thinking, 'mind' seemed the best choice.

The term that prompted most discussion was *to agathon*, the word with which Plato denoted the supreme Form, the spiritual analogue to the Sun in the visible world. When, as in Book 6, *agathon* is discussed in contrast with *kakon*, the darkness or ignorance of evil, we decided to stay with the conventional 'good' or 'goodness'. Occasionally, where some particular aspect of *to agathon* seems to be meant, we have used another translation appropriate to the context, but in these very few instances we have inserted *to agathon* in parentheses immediately after the term used. When the context suggested reference to the supreme reality itself, we felt that 'good' or 'goodness' would imply little more than a moral judgement. We decided in the end to follow Cicero, who translated *to agathon* into the Latin *Summum Bonum*, the Supreme Good. We hope this will suggest to the reader the highest reality in the cosmos; the true identity of every person and indeed of everything in the creation.

We have endeavoured to give the translation a freshness and vigour that will illuminate for today's reader the way these works drew and inspired listeners in antiquity and the Renaissance. We hope thus to open the mind to the eternal questions that these treatises address: What am I? What is this world around me? What is my relation to it?

March 1999
Clement Salaman
Dorine van Oyen
William D. Wharton

Translators' Note

In the translation that follows, lettered note references a, b, c, etc. refer to the Notes on the Greek Text on pp. 89-92. Numbered references 1, 2 etc. refer to the notes at the end of each book of the translation. There is no Book 15 (see p. 85).

The Corpus Hermeticum

Book 1
Poimandres to Hermes Trismegistus

1. Once, when mind had become intent on the things which are, and my understanding was raised to a great height, while my bodily senses were withdrawn as in sleep, when men are weighed down by too much food or by the fatigue of the body, it seemed that someone immensely great of infinite dimensions happened to call my name and said to me:

'What do you wish to hear and behold, and having beheld what do you wish to learn and know?'

2. 'Who are you?' said I.

He said, 'I am Poimandres the *Nous* of the Supreme. I know what you wish and I am with you everywhere.'

3. 'I wish to learn,' said I, 'the things that are and understand their nature and to know God. O how I wish to hear these things!'

He spoke to me again. 'Hold in your *Nous* all that you wish to learn and I will teach you.'

4. When he had thus spoken, he changed in form and forthwith, upon the instant, all things opened up before me; and I beheld a boundless view. All had become light, a gentle[a] and joyous light; and I was filled with longing when I saw it. After a little while, there had come to be in one part a downward moving darkness, fearful and loathsome, which I experienced as a twisting and enfolding motion. Thus it appeared to me.

I saw[b] the nature of the darkness change into a watery substance, which was indescribably shaken about, and gave out smoke as from fire, culminating in an unutterable and mournful echo. There was sent forth from the watery substance a loud, inarticulate cry; the sound, as I thought, was of the light[c].

5. Out of the light came forth the Holy Word which entered into the watery substance, and pure fire leapt from the watery substance and rose up; the fire was insubstantial, piercing and active. The air, being light, followed the breath, and mounted up till it reached the fire, away from earth and water, so that it seemed to be suspended from the fire. The earth and water remained in their own place mingled together, so that they could not be distinguished, and they were kept in motion by the breath of the Word, which passed over them within hearing.

6. Poimandres spoke to me and said:
    'Have you understood what you have seen and what it means?'
    'I shall come to know it,' I said.
    'That light,' he said, 'is I, *Nous*, your God, who was before the watery substance which appeared out of the darkness; and the clear Word from *Nous* is the Son of God.'
    'How can this be?' said I.
    'Know this,' he said. 'That which sees and hears within you is the Word of the Lord, and *Nous* is God the Father. They are not separate from each other, for their union is life.'
    'Thank you,' I said.
    'But perceive the light and know it,' said Poimandres.

7. And when he had thus spoken, he looked at me full in the face for a long time, so that his form made me tremble. When he had looked up, I saw in my own *Nous* that the light was in innumerable powers, having become an infinite world. I saw a fire encompassed by a mighty power, being under command to keep its place; I was intent upon these things, seeing them by means of the word of Poimandres.

8. As I stood amazed, Poimandres spoke again to me, saying:
    'You saw in *Nous* the first form, which is prior to the beginning of the beginningless and endless.' Thus spoke Poimandres to me.
    'Then,' I said, 'whence did the elements of nature have their origins?'
    He answered: 'From the will of God, which, holding the Word and seeing the beautiful cosmos made one exactly like it, fashioned from her own constituent elements and the offspring of souls.

9. 'Nous, God, being male and female, beginning as life and light, gave birth, by the Word, to another *Nous*, the Creator of the world; he, being the god of fire and air, formed seven powers who encompass in their circles the sensory world, and the governance of these powers is called destiny.

10. 'Immediately, the Word of God leapt forth from the downward moving elements to the pure work of the Creator, and was united with the Creator *Nous* (for he was of the same substance) and the downward moving elements of the creation were left behind, without the Word, to be matter alone.

11. 'Nous, the Creator, together with the Word, encompassing the spheres and spinning them round with a rushing motion, caused those things he had made to revolve and he allowed them to revolve from no fixed beginning to an end without limit, for it begins where it ends. The rotation of these spheres, as *Nous* willed, brought forth from the downward moving elements living beings without speech (for they did not contain the Word) and the air produced winged creatures and the water swimming creatures. The earth and the water were separated from each other, as *Nous* willed, and the earth brought forth from herself what she possesses, four-footed animals, reptiles, beasts; wild and tame.

12. 'Nous, the Father of all, who is life and light, brought forth Man, the same as himself, whom he loved as his own child, for Man was very beautiful, bearing the image of his Father. It was really his own form that God loved, and he handed over to him all his creation.

13. 'When Man had observed in the Father the creation of the Creator[d], he himself wished to create; and he was given permission to do so by the Father, being begotten in the sphere of the Creator, he observed carefully the creations of his brother from which[e] he obtained every power. The Father and the brother loved him, and each gave him of their own authority. Having acquired knowledge of their essence and partaking in their nature, he wished to break through the circumference of the spheres and to come to know the power of him who was set in authority over the fire.

14. 'Having all power over the world of mortals and living creatures without speech, he looked down through the harmony of the
cosmos and, having broken through the sovereignty[f] of the Divine
Power, he showed to downward moving Nature the beautiful form
of God.

'When she had seen the beauty[g] which never satiates of him who
had in himself all the energy of the powers and the form of God,
she smiled with love, because she had seen the image of the most
beautiful form of Man in the water and his shadow upon the earth.
He, seeing in himself[h] a similar form to his own in the water, fell
in love with her and wished to dwell there. No sooner wished than
done, and he inhabited a form without speech. Nature, having
taken her beloved, enfolded him completely and they united, for
they loved each other.

15. 'For this reason, of all living beings on earth, Man alone is
double: mortal because of the body, immortal because of the real
Man. For, although being immortal and having authority over all,
he suffers mortal things which are subject[i] to destiny. Then,
although above the harmony of the cosmos, he has become a slave
within it. He is beyond gender as he has been born from a Father
beyond gender; and he never sleeps as he is ruled by one who never
sleeps[j].'

16. 'And what after that, my *Nous*? For I love the conversation.'
Poimandres said: 'This is the mystery which has been kept
secret until this day. For Nature, united with Man, has brought
forth a wonder of wonders. Man, as[k] I told you, was of the Father[l]
and of spirit and had the nature of the harmony of the seven
spheres. So Nature did not wait, but immediately brought forth
seven men corresponding to the natures of the seven powers,
beyond gender and sublime.'
'And what after this, Poimandres? I greatly desire to hear more.
Please, do not stop.'
Poimandres said: 'Be silent, I have not yet fully expounded what
I have begun to say.'

17. 'Indeed, I shall say nothing,' said I.
'As I said, the generation of those seven took place in the
following way: the earth was female and the water potent and from

the fire came the fruit, and from the ether nature received the breath and produced the bodies according to the form of Man. From life and light Man became soul and *Nous*, from life soul, from light *Nous* and all things of the perceptible world remained so until the end of a cycle and the beginning of ages.

18. 'Listen further to the word you were longing to hear. On completion of the cycle, the bond of all was loosed according to the will of God, for all living beings, which were of both genders, were parted asunder at the same time as Man and became in turn male and female. God forthwith spoke the Holy Word: "All that has been fashioned and brought into being, may you increase and continue to increase, may you multiply and continue to multiply and may the man endowed with *Nous* recognise that he is immortal, that desire is the cause of death, and may he come to know all things that are."

19. 'God having thus spoken, Providence brought about acts of union through destiny and the harmony of the cosmos and established the generations and all things were multiplied according to their species. He who had recognised himself came to the Supreme Good, while he who had prized the body, born from the illusion of desire, remained wandering in the dark, suffering through the senses the things of death.'

20. 'In what terrible way do the ignorant go wrong,' said I, 'that they have been deprived of immortality?'
He said, 'You seem not to have taken heed of the things you have heard, did I not tell you to keep these things in mind?'
'Thank you,' I replied, 'I will do so and remember.'
He continued, 'If you have remembered, tell me, why are those who are in death, worthy of death?'
I replied, 'Because the grim darkness is the first origin of one's own body, from which darkness arose the watery nature, from which darkness[m] the body is formed in the sensory world of which death drinks.'

21. 'You have observed correctly,' he said. 'But why does he who has remembered himself go to the Father, as the Word of God says?'

I replied, 'Because the Father of all is constituted out of light
and life, whence Man has been begotten.'

Poimandres then said, 'The truth is[n]: light and life *is* God and
Father, whence Man is begotten. If, therefore, you realise yourself
as being from life and light and that you have been made out of
them, you will return to life.'

'But tell me further, how I shall return to life, my *Nous*? For God
declares: Let the man endowed with *Nous* remember himself.'

22. 'Do not all men have *Nous*?' I asked.

'Mark your words,' he replied. 'I, *Nous* itself, come to the aid of
the devout, the noble, pure, merciful, and those who live piously,
and my presence becomes a help, and straightaway they know all
things. By a life full of love they win the favour of the Father and
lovingly they give thanks, praising and singing hymns to him in
due order. Before giving up the body to its own death, they shut
down the senses, having seen their effects; or rather, I *Nous*, will
not allow the activities of the body which assail them to have
effect. Being the gatekeeper I shall close the entrances to evil and
dishonourable actions, cutting off their thoughts.

23. 'As for those without *Nous*, the evil, the worthless, the envious,
the greedy, murderers, the ungodly, I am very far from them,
having given way to the avenging spirit, who assaults each of them
through the senses, throwing fiery darts at them. He also moves
them to greater acts of lawlessness so that such a man suffers
greater retribution, yet he does not cease from having limitless
appetite for his lust nor from fighting in the dark without respite.
The avenging spirit then puts him to torture and increases the fire
upon him to its utmost.'

24. 'You have taught me these things well, as I wished, O *Nous*.
Now tell me how the way back is found?'

To this Poimandres replied: 'First, in the dissolution of the
material body, one gives[o] the body itself up to change. The form
you had becomes unseen, and you surrender to the divine power
your habitual character, now inactive. The bodily senses return to
their own sources. Then they become parts again and rise for
action, while the seat of emotions and desire go to mechanical
nature.

25. 'Thus a man starts to rise up through the harmony of the cosmos. To the first plain he surrenders the activity of growth and diminution; to the second the means of evil, trickery now being inactive; to the third covetous deceit, now inactive, and to the fourth the eminence pertaining to a ruler, being now without avarice; to the fifth impious daring and reckless audacity and to the sixth evil impulses for wealth, all of these being now inactive, and to the seventh plain the falsehood which waits in ambush.

26. 'Then, stripped of the activities of the cosmos, he enters the substance of the eighth plain with his own power, and he sings praises to the Father with those who are present; those who are near rejoice at his coming. Being made like to those who are there together, he also hears certain powers which are above the eighth sphere, singing praises to God with sweet voice. Then in due order, they ascend to the Father and they surrender themselves to the powers, and becoming the powers they are merged in God. This is the end, the Supreme Good, for those who have had the higher knowledge: to become God.

Well then, why do you delay? Should you not, having received all, become the guide to those who are worthy, so that the human race may be saved by God through you?'

27. Having said that to me, Poimandres mingled with the powers. When I had thanked and praised the Father of the All, I was freed by him, having been strengthened and instructed in the nature of all and in the most high vision, and I began to proclaim to men the beauty of piety and knowledge:

'O people, men born of the earth, who have given yourselves over to drink and sleep, and to ignorance of God, be sober, cease being intoxicated, cease being beguiled by dull sleep.'

28. Those who heard came to my side with one accord. I said: 'Why, O men born of earth, have you given yourselves over to death while having the power to partake of immortality? Repent. You who have kept company with those who have wandered and have shared in ignorance, be released from the dark light, take part in immortality. Put an end to destruction.'

29. Some of them kept on chattering and stood aloof, giving

themselves over to the path of death; others begged to be instructed, having thrown themselves at my feet. Lifting them up, I became the guide of the race, teaching the words of God, how they could be saved. I sowed in them the words of wisdom and they were nourished by the water of immortality. As the evening came and the rays of the sun began fully to set, I bade them to thank God; when they had fully given thanks each returned to his own bed.

30. I engraved in myself the beneficent kindness of Poimandres and having been filled with what I desired, I was delighted. For the sleep of the body became the sobriety of the soul, the closing of the eyes became true vision, my silence became pregnant with the Supreme Good, and the utterance of the Word became the generation of riches. All this came to me who had received it from my *Nous*, that is to say from Poimandres, the Word of the Supreme. I have come, divinely inspired by the truth. Wherefore, I give praise to God the Father with my whole soul and strength:

31.   Holy is God theᵖ Father of all.
      Holy is God whose will is accomplished by his own powers.
      Holy is God who wills to be known and is known by those
           that are his own.
      Holy art thou who by the Word has united all that is.
      Holy art thou of whom all Nature became an image.
      Holy art thou whom Nature has not created.
      Holy art thou who is stronger than all power.
      Holy art thou who art higher than all pre-eminence.
      Holy art thou who surpasses praises.

Receive pure offerings of speech offered to you by inner mind and heart, thou who art unutterable, vast, beyond description, who art spoken of by silence.

32. I beg you that I may not fall from the knowledge that leads towards our essence, and endow me with vitality; by this grace, I shall enlighten those of the race who are in ignorance, my brothers and your sons. Wherefore, I have faith and I bear witness. I go to life and light. You are blessed, Father. He who is your man wants to share in your holiness, as you have given him all authority.

Book 2
Hermes to Asclepius[1]

1. H – Is not everything that is moved, O Asclepius, moved in something and by something?

A – Certainly.

H – Must not that in which something is moved be greater than what is moved?

A – It must.

H – Must not the mover be more powerful than the moved?

A – Definitely more powerful.

H – And must not that in which movement occurs have a nature opposite to that of the moved?

A – Yes, indeed.

2. H – Now this cosmos is vast. Surely there is not a greater body than this?

A – Agreed.

H – And it is dense? For it is filled with many other great bodies, or rather with all bodies that exist.

A – That is so.

H – Is the cosmos a body?

A – It is.

H – Is it moved?

3. A – Certainly.

H – Then how large must be the space in which the cosmos is moved and what is the nature of that space? Must it not be much larger, in order to accommodate the continuous course of the movement of the cosmos and to prevent its motion from being hindered by its confinement?

A – It must be something huge, O Trismegistus.

4. H – What is it like? Must it not be of an opposite nature, Asclepius? And the nature opposite to body is bodiless.

A – Agreed.

H – The space then, is bodiless. The bodiless is either divine or it is God. I understand 'divine' to mean not 'begotten' but 'unbegotten'.

5. If the bodiless is divine it is endowed with being; if it is God it stands apart from being, otherwise, it would be perceptible. For us God is the highest perception, but not for Him. For that which is perceived is perceived by the senses of the perceiver; therefore, God is not perceived by Himself. However, in that He is not other than that which is perceived, He does perceive Himself.

6. To us He is something separate and it is because of this that we perceive Him. But if the space in which the cosmos is moved is perceived, it is not God[a] but simply space[b]. If the space is God[c], it is no longer space, but that which encompasses all activity. All that is moved is not moved in what is moved, but in what is unmoved. The mover is still; it is impossible for Him[d] to be moved.

A – How then, O Trismegistus, are these things here moved by those which move them? For you have said that the planetary spheres are moved by the fixed stars.

H – It is not the same movement[e], O Asclepius, but a movement in the opposite direction, for they are not moved in the same way, but in a way opposite to each other. This countermovement has a point for its movement that is fixed.

7. For countermovement is the bringer of stillness[f]. Now the planetary spheres are moved in the opposite direction to the fixed stars. They are moved by each other in opposition. They are moved round their opposite by a point which is fixed and it cannot be otherwise. Those two Bears [the constellations which you see] neither set nor rise and are turned about the same point, do you think they are moved or are fixed?

A – They are moved, O Trismegistus.

H – With what kind of movement, Asclepius?

A – With a movement that turns around that point[g].

H – The circular movement is a movement about that point[h] governed by that which is still, for revolution round that point prevents any digression; digression is prevented, if the revolution is established. Thus the movement in the opposite direction is stabilising and is fixed by the principle of countermovement.

8. I shall give you an example upon earth under your very eyes. Look at mortal beings, for instance a man swimming. The water

flows, but the counteraction of feet and hands provide stability for the man, so that he is not carried down stream.

A – A very clear example, Trismegistus.

H. – All movement then is produced in that which does not move and by that which does not move. Therefore, the movement of the cosmos and of all living material turns out not to arise from what comes from outside the cosmos[i] but from what is within, which moves outward[j]: from the soul, from the breath of life or from another incorporeal being. For a body does not move a body that has a soul, nor in general any body even if it has no soul.

9. A – How can you say this, Trismegistus? Cannot pieces of wood, stones and other things that have no soul move bodies?

H – Not so, Asclepius. When a body moves something without a soul, it is that within, not the body, which moves both the bearer and what is borne.

Hence a body with a soul, when it moves, moves that which is inert[k]. Therefore you see the soul is weighed down whenever on its own it carries two bodies. Clearly then, things which are moved are moved in something and by something.

10. A – Must objects be moved in something[l], O Trismegistus?

H – They must[m], Asclepius. Nothing which is, is a void; only non-existence is void, being foreign to existence. For the existing can never be void.

A – But are there not some things which are void, O Trismegistus, such as an empty jar, an empty pot, a whole river bed and other similar things?[n]

H – What a huge mistake, Asclepius! What is totally full and quite enormous[o] you have simply taken as empty.

11. A – How can you say this, O Trismegistus?

H – Is air a substance, Asclepius?

A – It is.

H – Does not this substance pervade all that exists, and in pervading all does it not fill it? Is this substance not a mixture of substances[p]? Therefore, are not all things which you say are void filled with air? Therefore, those things which you say are void one should call hollow, not void. The fact is that they are full of air and the breath of life.

27

12. Your words are irrefutable, O Trismegistus. So what shall we say is the space in which everything is moved?

H – It is bodiless, Asclepius.

A – But what is the bodiless?

H – *Nous*, the Word[q], emerging out of that which is whole, entire and complete; *Nous* containing itself, unembodied, steadfast, unaffected, and impalpable, itself standing by itself, containing and preserving all beings, whose[r] glories are the Supreme Good, truth, the origin of breath, the origin of soul.

A – What then is God?

H – He is not any one of these, but He is the cause of their existence, the cause of the existence of everything and of every individual.

13. He has left no space for the unreal. All that is has come from the real and not from the unreal. The quality of the unreal is that it cannot come into existence, indeed it cannot become anything. Again the real never has the nature of the unreal.

14. A – What do you mean by: 'never has the nature of the unreal?'

H – God is *Nous* and the cause of existence; He is not breath, but the cause of the breath's existence; He is not light, but the cause of the light's existence. Thus one should worship God by these two names (*Nous* and the cause of existence), since they belong to Him alone and to no one else. No other beings spoken of as gods, men or divine powers can be even in the slightest degree good, but God alone. God is this alone and nothing else. All other things are contained[s] within the nature of the Supreme Good, for they are body and soul, but themselves have no place to contain the Supreme Good.

15. The greatness of this good is such that it is the reality of all beings; of the bodily and of the bodiless, of the sensory and of the subtle. This is the Supreme Good, this is God. Therefore, do not call anything else good since then you blaspheme, and do not ever call God anything but good, since then again you blaspheme.

16. Everyone uses the term 'good', but what it is, not everyone perceives. On account of this, God is not perceived by everyone, but in ignorance they call gods and certain men good who can never be

and never become good. The Supreme Good is not at all alien to God; it is inseparable from Him, as it is God Himself. All the other immortal gods are honoured by the name of God. However, God is good, not by being honoured, but by his nature. For the nature of God is one: supreme goodness; God and goodness are one generative power, from which come all generations. He who gives all and takes nothing is good. God gives all and takes nothing. So God is the Supreme Good and the Supreme Good is God.

17. The other name is that of the Father, by virtue of Him being the author of all things; for the Father's nature is to create. Therefore, the raising of children[2] is held in the greatest esteem in life and most blessed by right-thinking people; and the greatest misfortune and impiety is when someone departs from mankind without children, for he suffers punishment after death from the divine powers. This is the retribution: that the soul without children is condemned to a body that is neither male nor female, and is cursed by the sun. Therefore, Asclepius, do not congratulate anyone without children but rather take pity on his misfortune, knowing what punishment awaits him. Let this much be spoken as a foretaste to the understanding of the nature of the All.

*

1. There is substantial evidence that a portion of the opening of Book 2 of the *Corpus Hermeticum* as well as an entire intervening book have been lost from the manuscripts. In manuscripts that contain titles for individual treatises, Book 2 is labelled *A Universal Teaching of Hermes to Tat*. What follows in the manuscripts, however, is addressed to Asclepius, suggesting that at an early point, a treatise was lost. Additional evidence for omission comes from Johannes Stobaeus, whose AD 500 anthology of ancient wisdom and literature for his son's education contains extensive excerpts from this treatise. One excerpt of some twenty-five lines ends with a phrase identical with the first line of the manuscripts' Book 2, is addressed to Asclepius, and matches the rest of the treatise in subject matter. This fragment is, therefore, generally regarded as four Book 2 chapters that precede the opening extant in the manuscripts. It is also unlikely that the abrupt beginning of the Stobaean excerpt corresponds to the opening of the original treatise. If one assumes that pages were lost between the original Book 2 (*Universal Teaching of Hermes to Tat*) and the manuscripts' Book 2 (Hermes to Asclepius), one can also assume that the original beginning of Book 2 was also lost. For a fuller discussion of

the Stobaean fragments, see Scott, vol. I, pp. 82-6, and NF, vol. I, pp.
xli-xlvi. For the problem of the opening of Book 2, see Scott, vol. II, p. 75.

2. The meaning here of *paidopoia* is 'spiritual children'. cf. 'On the
Ogdoad and the Ennead' in *NH*.

Book 3

1. God is the glory of all things, the divine being and the divine
nature. God, *Nous*, nature and matter are the origin of beings. God
is wisdom for the revelation of all things. The divine being is the
origin, as is also nature, power of movement, necessity, completion, and renewal. For in the abyss was infinite darkness, water
and fine intelligent spirit. By the power of God were these within
the chaos. A holy light was sent forth, and the elements from the
watery substance solidified under the earth. All the gods divided
the seed-bearing nature amongst themselves.

2. All beings were undefined and unwrought, the light elements
were then separated off and raised on high, and the heavy were
founded firmly upon the watery sand. All was distinguished by
fire, all was raised up to be supported by the breath of life. The
vault of heaven appeared in seven circles, and the gods appeared
in the form of stars with all their constellations, and heaven with
the gods was complete in every detail. The universe was encompassed by air and sustained on its circular course by divine spirit.

3. Each god sent forth by his own power what had been appointed
to him. There came into being four-footed animals, reptiles, fish
and fowl; all prolific seed, and herb and the shoot of every flower.
These had within themselves the seed of regeneration. The gods
sent forth the generations of men, so that they should know the
works of God, be the active witness of nature, and that they should
multiply, rule over all under heaven, and know what is good; and
so that they should increase and continue to increase, multiply
and continue to multiply. Through their own wonder-working
course the gods sent forth every soul clothed in flesh, so that men
should survey heaven, the paths of the heavenly gods, the works
of God and the activity of nature; so that they should know the
signs of what is good, the power of God, and the turning fate of
good and evil things and discover all the marvellous works of good
men.

4. So men began to live and understand the destiny assigned to them by the course of the circling gods, and they were dissolved in what they were, leaving great memorials of their work on earth; their name remains until the darkening of ages. And every generation of embodiment, and also the seeds of the fruit and of every work of art will perish, but will be increased by necessity and renewed by the gods and by the course of nature's measured cycle. The whole blending of the cosmos renewed by nature is of God. For nature is also seated in God.

Book 4
Hermes to Tat

1. H – Since the Creator made the whole cosmos, not with hands but by the Word, understand that he is present and always is, creating all things, being one alone, and by his will producing all beings. For such is his body: intangible, invisible, immeasurable, indivisible, like nothing else[a]. It is not fire, nor water, nor air, nor breath, but through it all things exist[b].

2. Being supremely good, he set it up in dedication to that One alone[c], and he wished to adorn the earth as the form of the body of God. He sent down man, a mortal being, from an immortal being. The cosmos rules over the life[d] of living beings and man rules over the cosmos by means of speech and *Nous*. For man became the witness of God's work, and he worshipped the Creator and came to know him.

3. Therefore, O Tat, God has given the Word to all men to partake in, but not so with *Nous*. He was not jealous, for jealousy of any one[e] does not originate from there, but is created in the souls of men who have no *Nous*.

    T – Then why, O father, has God not given to everyone a share of *Nous*?

    H – He willed, my son, to set it up as a prize before souls.

4. T – And where did he set it up?

    H – He filled a great bowl with *Nous* and sent it down, and he appointed a herald to make this announcement to the hearts of men:

'Plunge into this bowl, if you can, having faith that you will rise to him that sent down the bowl, realising why you came into being.'

Those who heard the proclamation, merged with *Nous*, partook of higher knowledge and became perfect and complete, since they had received *Nous*. Those who missed the proclamation had the Word, but had not received *Nous*, ignorant as they were as to why they were born, and from whom.

5. The perceptions of these people are like those of dumb animals, having a mixture of rage and lust, they do not value things worthy of their attention, but turn to the pleasures and appetites of the body, believing that man was born for that reason. Those who partook in the gift of God, O Tat, are immortal rather than mortal, if one considers their works. They comprehend all in their *Nous*: whatever is on earth, in heaven, and beyond heaven. Having thus raised themselves, they see the Supreme Good, and realising that, they regard time spent here as a misfortune. Disregarding the gross and the subtle, they hasten to the One alone.

6. This, Tat, is the knowledge of *Nous*, and the vision of what comes from God. It is the perception of God, since the bowl is of God.

T – I also wish to be immersed in *Nous*, O father.

H – If you don't first hate your body, son, you cannot love your Self. If you love your Self you will have *Nous*, and having *Nous* you will partake of knowledge.

T – Why do you say that, father?

H – For, son, it is impossible to be governed by both, by the mortal and by the divine. There are two kinds of beings, the embodied and unembodied, in whom there is the mortal and the divine spirit. Man is left to choose one or the other, if he so wishes. For one cannot choose both at once; when one is diminished, it reveals the power of the other.

7. Thus this power, the choice of the better, not only happens to be the most glorious for him who chooses, in that it unites man with God, but it also shows reverence to God. The inferior choice has destroyed man. Nothing offends God but this: as processions passing in the road cannot achieve anything themselves, yet still

obstruct others, so these men merely process through the universe, led by the pleasures of the body.

8. These things being so, Tat, the things of God have always belonged and will always belong to us. May what comes from us accord with that and may there be no delay. Since God is not the cause of evils, we are to blame, preferring these things to what is good. Do you see, O son, how many bodies we have to pass through, how many bands of demons, through how many series of repetitions and cycles of the stars, before we hasten to the One alone? All this has to be crossed[f]; the Supreme Good is unlimited, and it has no beginning and no end. But to us it appears that knowledge has a beginning.

9. Knowledge then is not the origin of the Supreme Good, but for us it provides the origin of what is to be known. Let us therefore take hold of the origin, and pass over everything else with speed; for it is a path full of tangles, when leaving the familiar and present, to return to the ancient and original. For what appears to the eyes delights us, and what is unseen makes us mistrust. To those who have eyes, evil is most evident and the Supreme Good is hidden. For the Supreme Good has no form and leaves no mark. Thus it is like to itself, but unlike all else. What is unembodied, can never be seen by a body.

10. This is the difference between the like and the unlike, and the inferiority of the unlike compared to the like. For the One is the origin and the root of all, and nothing is without origin. The origin arises only from itself, because it is the origin of all other things; for it is itself, because it does not come from another origin. Therefore the One is the origin and comprehends all[g] by number, without being comprehended by any number, and being the producer of all things by number, is not itself produced by any other number.

11. Everything that comes into being is imperfect and undetermined[h]; it may be increased and diminished, but no such thing happens to the perfect. And what can grow, grows by virtue of the One, but is overpowered by its own weakness, no longer able to give way to the One. This is the image of God, O Tat, that has been drawn for you, as far as it can be. If you observe it clearly and

reflect upon it with the eyes of the heart, believe me, my son, you will find the way to higher things. In fact the image itself will guide you. For sight of the image has a special quality of its own. It dwells in those who have already seen it and draws them upward, just as they say a magnet draws up iron.

Book 5
Hermes to Tat

1. This teaching also I shall fully expound to you, O Tat, so that you are not shut off from God who is too great for a name. Understand that what appears unmanifest to many will become most evident to you, for it would not exist if it were not manifest to you. Everything that is manifest has been brought into being; for it has been brought to light. However, the unmanifest exists always; it does not need to appear, for it exists always and it makes everything else manifest, though it itself is unmanifest since it always is. That which makes manifest is not itself made manifest, for it has not been brought forth. But it brings all images to the mind in imagination. Things that are begotten belong only to imagination. For imagination is nothing but begetting[a].

2. It is plain that the One is unborn and not imagined and it is unmanifest, but it appears as all kinds of images, through all and in all and chiefly to those to whom it wishes to appear. My son, Tat, pray first to the Lord and Father; he is single, but not the One, apart from whom is the One. Pray that through grace you will be able to perceive God as so great that even[b] just one ray of Him may shine in your mind. For pure perception perceives the unmanifest, as it is itself also unmanifest. If you are strong enough, He will appear to the eye of *Nous*, O Tat. For the Lord appears in His bounty throughout the whole universe. Can you see pure perception and take hold of it with these hands and contemplate the image of God? But if you cannot see what is within, how can God who is Himself within you appear to you through your eyes?

3. If you wish to see Him, consider the sun, the course of the moon, the order of the stars. Who watches over this order? For all order sets a limit by number and place. The sun is the greatest god of the gods in heaven, for whom all heavenly gods give way as to a

king and master. He, who is so great, greater than the earth and
the sea, supports the turning stars. He has them above him
although they are smaller than himself. Does he stand in awe of
any one? Does he fear anyone, O son? Does not each of those stars
which are in heaven, follow a similar if not identical course? Who
has ordained to each the direction and size of its course?

4. This Great Bear turns around itself, and carries the whole
universe along with itself. Who has acquired that as an instrument? Who has thrown boundaries round the sea? Who has set the
earth in place? For there is someone, O Tat, who is the creator and
master of all these things. It is impossible that the place, the
number and the measure be preserved, without him who created
it. For all order is created, and what is out of place and out of
measure is not created; but not even that, my son, is without a
master. For if the disorder is in need of order, when so to speak, it
stops the normal working of order, it is nevertheless under a
master, albeit one who has not yet brought it within the bounds of
order.

5. O that you could grow wings and fly up into the air, and that,
poised between earth and heaven, you might see the firmness of
earth, the liquidity of the sea, the course of the rivers and the free
flow of the air, the piercing fire, the revolution of the stars, the
swiftness of the heavenly movement encircling all these things.
What most blessed vision, O son, to behold all that in one moment;
the unmoving being moved, the unmanifest being made manifest
through what it creates! This is the very order of the universe and
this is the beauty of the order.

6. If you also wish to see God through mortal beings who are on
earth and in the sea, consider, my son, man being formed in the
womb and examine carefully the skill of God's work, and understand who creates this beautiful and godlike image of man? Who
has outlined the eyes? Who has pierced out the nostrils and ears?
Who has opened the mouth? Who has stretched and fastened the
sinews? Who has conducted the veins in their channels? Who has
strengthened the bones, and covered the flesh with skin? Who has
separated the fingers? Who has widened the soles of the feet? Who
has bored the passages through the body, who has stretched out

the spleen? Who has shaped the heart like a pyramid and joined the sinews together? Who has broadened the liver? Who has hollowed out the lungs and made the stomach capacious? Who has fashioned the most honourable parts so that they may be seen and concealed those parts which are unseemly?

7. See how many skills arise from one substance and how many forms are made by one impression; and all things beautiful, all things measured, all things varied. Who made all these? What mother, what father, if not the unmanifest God, who created all things by His own will?

8. No one says that a statue or a portrait has come into being without a sculptor or a painter; then has this work come into being without a creator? What blindness! What sacrilege! What mindless arrogance! My son Tat, never deprive the works of creation of their creator. He is greater than anything the name of God implies, so great is the Father of all; for He is single and His work is just this: to be Father.

9. If you force me to speak more boldly, it is His nature to conceive all things and create them; and as without the Creator nothing can come into existence, so He would not exist eternally if He had not always been creating all things in heaven, in air, in earth, in the sea, everywhere in the universe, everywhere in the All, in what is and what is not. There is nothing in all this which is not Himself[c]. Both the things that are and the things that are not are himself. For the things that are, He has made manifest and the things that are not He contains within Himself.

10. This is God, greater than a name. He is unmanifest, yet He is most manifest; He can be perceived by *Nous*; He can be seen by the eyes. He is bodiless, yet He has many bodies, or rather every body. Nothing is which He is not. For He is all that exists and He has therefore all names, because all names come from one Father, and that is why He Himself has no name, for he is the Father of all. How[d] can you be praised to others or to yourself? And where shall I look to praise you: above, below, inside or outside? For you there is no direction, no place, nor any other being. All is within you, all

comes from you. You give everything and take nothing. For you have everything and there is nothing you do not have.

11. When shall I sing your praises? For it is not possible to find your hour or your season. For what shall I praise you? For what you have created or for what you have not created? For what you have revealed or for what you have hidden? And why shall I praise you? Because you are of my own nature? Because you have what is your own? Because you are other? But you are whatsoever I am; you are whatever I do; you are whatever I speak. You are all things and there is nothing else. Even what is not you are. You are all that has come into being; you are what has not come into being. You are *Nous*, and what is apprehended by *Nous*; you are Father as you create, God as you are in every action, the Supreme Good as you are the cause of all.

The finest part of matter is air, of air, soul, of soul, *Nous*, of *Nous*, God.[1]

*

1. A prayer-like formula, which is repeated in Book 12.

Book 6
Hermes to Asclepius

1. The Supreme Good, O Asclepius, is not in anything, if not in God alone, rather, the Supreme Good is always God Himself. If this is so, it is the real nature of all movement and of all generation. Nothing is bereft of this real nature which has[a] an energy that brings things to rest round itself. It is not in want and has no excess; it is completely full and supplies all needs; it is in the beginning of all things. For in saying that the provider of everything is good I am saying that it is always good in every way.

This Supreme Good belongs to nothing else but to God alone. For He lacks nothing, lest any desire to possess anything may render Him evil, nor can anything be lost to Him which would make Him grieve, for grief is the heritage of evil. No being is mightier than God, by whom He could be treated as an enemy, nor is it possible for Him to suffer any injustice by anyone and therefore He will love everyone. No being is disobedient to Him which would provoke His anger, nor is any being wiser which would provoke His jealousy.

2. Since none of these afflictions belong to being, what is left but the Supreme Good alone? For just as none of them belong to being, so this Good will not be found in any of these afflictions. But all these other afflictions exist in every being: in the small and in the great, in individual creatures and in that living being himself (the cosmos), which is greater and more powerful than all beings and all things. What is born is full of suffering, for birth itself is suffering; and when there is suffering the Supreme Good is never there; and when this Good is there, there is no suffering at all. Where there is day there is no night, where there is night there is no day. Therefore the Supreme Good cannot be in what is begotten, but only in what is unbegotten. Just as there is provision of everything in the physical world, likewise the Supreme Good permeates abundantly. In this way the cosmos is good, as it creates all things; it is good with regard to its creative aspect, but in everything else it is not good. For it is subject to suffering and movement and is the producer of beings who are destined to suffer.

3. Within man the Supreme Good is limited by the measure of evil. For in man just a little evil is counted as good. Good for him is the smallest portion of evil. Therefore for him, good cannot be free from evil. For in man goodness is ill-used, and when it is ill-used goodness no longer remains and when it does not remain, evil is born. Therefore the Supreme Good is only in God, or rather God himself is this Good. Thus O Asclepius, there is only the term 'good' for men, never its reality; for that is impossible. The gross body allows no room for it, bound fast everywhere by evil, toils, pains, desires, passions, deceits, foolish opinions. And, Asclepius, the worst of all is that each of these things which have just been mentioned, are in man considered to be the greatest good, whereas in fact each is an unsurpassable evil. Greed, the root of all evil, is the error of man; it is the absence of goodness.

4. And I am thankful to God for putting even a taste of the knowledge of the Supreme Good into my *Nous*, because this Good cannot exist in the world. For the world is the sum total of evil;

God the unlimited goodness, or rather goodness the limitless God. For the excellencies of beautiful things are round His true nature, and appear in some way even more pure and simple, for they are of God. One must have courage to say, O Asclepius, that the essence of God, if indeed He has an essence, is beauty; but no[b] beauty and goodness are to be found in the things of the cosmos. For all things which fall under the eye are images and, as it were, paintings. But what does not fall under the eye is chiefly the excellence of beauty and goodness. And just as the eye cannot see God, so it cannot see beauty and goodness. For these are the attributes of God, perfect and complete, belonging to Him alone, they are His very own, inseparable and most beloved; either God loves them or they love God.

5. If you can perceive God, you will perceive beauty, goodness (*to agathon*) and splendour, illumined by God. That beauty is incomparable and that goodness inimitable, as is God Himself. Thus insofar as you perceive God, you must perceive beauty and goodness. These are not shared by other living beings, as they are inseparable from God. If you seek after God, you also seek after beauty. There is one way leading to that beauty: devotion with knowledge.

6. Thus the ignorant and those not on the way of devotion dare to speak of a man as beautiful and good; however, man in his dream, can by no means see if anything is good but he takes every evil to himself; believing evil to be good, and thus using it for himself, he becomes insatiable and fearful of being robbed of it; he struggles for everything, not only to have it but to increase it. Such things are good and beautiful to men, O Asclepius, and we can neither escape them nor hate them. The worst thing of all is that we have need of these things and we cannot live without them.

Book 7

1. Whither are you being carried, O men, drunk as you are, having swallowed neat, the word of ignorance, which you cannot keep down, but are already vomiting up? Stop, be sober. Look up with the eyes of the heart; and if all of you cannot, at least those who can. The evil of ignorance floods the whole earth and completely

destroys the soul confined to the body, not allowing it to be brought to a safe harbour.

2. Therefore don't be carried down by the great flood, but make use of the tide. Let those of you who can find the safe harbour bring your ship in, and seek one who will lead you by the hand to the gates of the knowledge in your heart. There is the bright light, clear of darkness, where no one gets drunk, but all are sober, looking with the heart to Him who wills to be seen. He cannot be heard, He cannot be uttered, nor seen by the eyes, but by *Nous* and the heart. First, you have to strip off the garment which you are wearing, the web of ignorance, the fabric of evil, the knot of destruction, the girdle of darkness, the living death, the sentient corpse, the portable tomb, the robber in your house, him who hates through what he loves and bears malice through what he hates.

3. Such is the hateful garment you wear, which binds you down in itself lest, when you look up and see the beauty of truth and the Supreme Good which lies within, you should hate the evil of this garment and realise its treachery. This has ensnared you, making the seeming senses, which are not acknowledged, insensible; for it has blocked them up with much gross matter and filled them with loathsome pleasure, so that you do not hear what you should hear and do not see what you should see.

Book 8
Hermes to Tat

1. Now, my son, we must speak about the soul and the body: in what way the soul is immortal, and what is the activity which forms the body and dissolves it. Mortality has nothing to do with this. The concept comes from the word 'immortal'. Either mortality is a meaningless word or it has lost its first syllable, as it is pronounced 'mortal' instead of 'immortal'. Mortality is a kind of destruction, but nothing in the universe is destroyed. If the second God is the cosmos, an immortal being, it is impossible for any part of an immortal being to die. Everything in the cosmos is a part of the cosmos, but especially man, the living being with speech.

2. The first God of all is in fact eternal, unbegotten and the Creator

of all. The second God is in the image of the first. He is begotten by Him and he is within Him and by Him he is sustained and made immortal; thus, by his own[a] Father he is ever-living as an immortal. What goes on living is distinct from the eternal. The eternal was not begotten from another. You might say that He was begotten from Himself, if so, He was never begotten, but He is always coming into being; He is the eternal. Because of Him the All is eternal. The Father is eternal because of Himself, but the cosmos is eternal and immortal, because it is begotten of the Father.

3. And however much material there was, it being subject to His disposal, the Father turned it all into a body. He raised it up and made it spherical, conferring this quality on what He had wrought: namely an immortal and eternal materiality. When He had sown certain kinds of causal forms into the sphere, He enclosed them as within a cavern. As He wished to adorn the material within Himself with all qualities, He invested the whole body with immortality, so that this material would not wish itself separate from its composition with the body, and thus dissolve into its own undifferentiated state. When this material was not a body it was undifferentiated, my son. In this world other small things, such as growth and diminution, which men call death are enveloped by this material.

4. This undifferentiated state exists in respect of earthly beings. The bodies of the celestials have one order which was assigned to them by the Father in the beginning; and this indestructible order is kept unbroken by the periodic return of each body in the cosmic cycle. Within that cycle earthly bodies are formed, returned and dissolved into bodies that are indestructible, that is immortal. Thus there is deprivation of the senses but no destruction of bodies.

5. The third living being, man, has been begotten in the image of the cosmos, but, as the Father willed, not[b] living like other earthly creatures. Not only does he have affinity with the second God, but also a conception of the first. He perceives the second God as a body, the first he conceives as without a body and as *Nous*, that is the Supreme Good.

T – Then does this being, man, not die?

H – Be still, my son, and consider what is God, what is the cosmos, what being is immortal, what is dissolved and consider that the cosmos is made by God and in God, man is made by the cosmos and in the cosmos, and that God is the source, the boundary and the constitution of everything.

Book 9
Hermes to Asclepius

1. Yesterday, O Asclepius, I spoke about the teaching as a whole; now I consider it necessary to follow that and speak in detail about the subject of sense perception. The sensory perception and understanding may seem to differ: one is connected with matter and the other with being. To me they both seem to be one and without difference; I mean in man. For in other living beings sense is one with nature, but there is understanding in man. *Nous* differs as much from understanding as God does from divinity. Divinity comes from God, as understanding, being akin to the Word, comes from *Nous*. In fact understanding and the Word are instruments of each other, for neither is the Word spoken without understanding nor does understanding appear without the Word.

2. Now sense and understanding both flow together in man, as they are entwined with each other. It is neither possible to understand without sense nor to sense without understanding. Is it possible to understand without sense, even when people imagine visible objects in dreams?ª For it seems to me that both these activities have taken place in the dream vision, since they are both aroused in sense which partly belongs to the body and partly to the soul; and whenever both parts of sense are in unison, understanding arises, being born from *Nous*.

3. *Nous* brings forth all concepts, good ones when it receives the seed from God, and the opposite when it receives them from one of the demons, there being no part of the cosmos that is free from demons. As the demon receives its illumination from God, it steals in and sows the seed of his own workings, and *Nous* brings to birth what has been sown: adultery, murder, violence to one's father, sacrilege, ungodliness, strangling, suicide from a cliff and all such other demonic actions.

4. Few are the seeds of God, but they are mighty, beautiful and good: virtue, self-control and devotion to God. Devotion to God is knowledge of God. He who has discovered it, is filled with all that is good, and he is endowed with divine understanding, which is not like the understanding of the multitude. Therefore, those who are seated in knowledge neither please the multitude nor does the multitude please them. They seem to be mad and have become a laughing stock; they are hated and despised and may even be put to death. Evil, we say[b], must needs live down here in its own country. Its country is the earth, but not the cosmos as some blasphemously affirm. However, the man who fears God will support all since he has realised true knowledge; for to such a man all things are good, even those that are evil for others. When entangled with difficulties he refers all things to true knowledge; he alone turns evil into good.

5. I return again to the subject of sense perception. For to use the senses with understanding is the property of man. But, as I said before, not every man is capable of understanding, for one kind of man is concerned with material things and another with being. As I have said, the materialist, in the midst of evil, receives the seed of his understanding from the demons; the other men, surrounded by goodness, are in their being preserved by God. God, the Creator of all things, in creating them creates them in the likeness of Himself; as they have been made good, he keeps them in view[c] while they perform their activities. The friction of the cosmos produces different kinds of generations, making some foul by evil, purifying others by goodness. The cosmos, O Asclepius, has its own sense and understanding, not such as in man, not diversified, but more excellent and simple.

6. For the sense perception and understanding of the cosmos are one; they are an instrument of God's will to create[d] all things and to return them to that one. The cosmos was in fact made an instrument for creating all beings within itself fit for its use by preserving within itself all the seeds which it had received from God. It was made an instrument for renewing all beings by dissolving them; and, like the good farmer of life, for offering to bring them, once dissolved, renewal through transformation. There is nothing to which He does not give life. He gives life to things by

moving them. At one and the same time He is space and the Creator of life.

7. The bodies made from matter are diverse. Some are from earth, some from water, some from air, some from fire. All is compounded of parts, some more complex, others simpler. The more complex are heavier, and the simpler lighter. The rapid motion of the turning cosmos produces the varied qualities of beings. The blast of air from this is continuous and lends qualities to bodies as well as the abundance of life.

8. God is the Father of the cosmos, the cosmos is the father of those within the cosmos, the cosmos is the son of God, and those within the cosmos have been created by the cosmos. The cosmos has been aptly-named 'order'; for it gives order to all things through the diversity of their origin and the continuity of life, through untiring activity and the speed of desire, through the shadow[e] of the elements and the giving of order to what comes into being. That it should be called 'order' is both necessary and fitting. Thus the sense perception and understanding of all that lives come in from outside. They breathe by means of that which contains them, but the cosmos receives sense perception and understanding once and for all at the time it was born and having received them from God it keeps them.

9. But God is not, as some will think, without sense perception and without understanding. Through their very piety such men blaspheme; for, O Asclepius, all things that exist are in God. They have been brought forth by God and depend upon Him. Some work through bodies, others make things move through the soul; some lend life through breath, others receive the dead remains. All this is just. I should rather say that God does not contain these beings, but to tell the truth, He is them all. He does not take them in from outside but issues them out. This is the sense perception and understanding of God: ever to move all beings, and there will never be a time when anything will be left without Him. Whenever I speak of beings, I speak of God, for God supports beings and nothing is outside Him and He outside nothing.

10. O Asclepius, these things will seem true to you if you under-

stand them, but if you remain ignorant they are beyond belief. To understand them is to take them as true, and not to understand them is to take them as untrue. My discourse leads[f] to the truth; the mind is great, and guided by this teaching may arrive at the truth. When the mind has comprehended all things and found them to be in harmony with what has been expounded by the teaching, it takes them to be true and comes to rest in that beautiful truth. Those who understand through God hold what has just been spoken to be true, but those who do not understand do not believe it. Let this much be said about understanding and sense perception.

Book 10
Hermes to Tat

1. I imparted yesterday's discourse to you, O Asclepius, so today it is right to give it to Tat, especially because it is an abridgement of the general[a] teaching addressed to him. God, Father and the Supreme Good have the same nature, or rather power. The name of nature also means growth, as it concerns beings which change and which are both movable and immovable: it concerns the divine and the human, both of which God wills into being. We have discussed power elsewhere and also other divine and human matters, which have to be kept in mind on this subject.

2. The power of God is his will and God's essence is to will all things to be. What is God, Father and the Supreme Good but the existence of all things even those that are not, what else but the very substance[b] of all that is? This is God, this is Father and this is the Supreme Good; without any further addition. Although the cosmos and the sun are father to them that partake of them, they are not in the same manner the cause of the Supreme Good in living beings, nor of their life. If they are father they are wholly controlled by the will of the Supreme Good, without which nothing can be or become.

3. The father is the cause of his children, both of their generation and their nourishment, having received the desire from the Supreme Good through the sun, for this Good is the creative principle. This cannot be present in anyone but that One alone, which

takes nothing but wills all things to be. I do not therefore say, Tat, that the One creates; for over a long period of time the creator is defective, in that sometimes he creates and sometimes he does not. Sometimes he is defective in quality and at other times in quantity. Sometimes he creates many things of a particular kind and sometimes their opposite. But God, Father and the Supreme Good are there for the existence of all.

4. These things are so for the man who is able to see; God wills this and so it is; indeed it is for this man's sake. One might even say all other things exist for his sake. It is the nature of the Supreme Good that this Good should be known, O Tat.

T. – O father, you have filled us with a good and most beautiful vision so that my mind's eye is almost afraid of such a sight.

H. – It does not, like the rays of the sun, which are fiery, blaze on the eyes and make them close. This is the vision of the Supreme Good; it shines forth in such a way that the man who has the power can as far as possible perceive the flowing light of pure perception. Not only does it come down[c] to us more swiftly, but it is harmless and is wholly immortal.

5. Indeed, those who are able to drink in more of this vision often lose awareness of the body in this most beautiful sight as happened to our ancestors Ouranos and Cronos.

T. – May that happen to us, O father!

H. – May it indeed, my son. But as yet we are too weak in sight and are not strong enough[d] to open the eyes of the mind and to behold the beauty of that Supreme Good, incorruptible and incomprehensible. When you have nothing to say about it, then you will see it; for the experience of it is the silence of God and the withdrawal of all the senses.

6. He who has perceived it, cannot perceive any other; he who has contemplated it cannot contemplate any other; he cannot hear of any other, he cannot even move the body. Ceasing[e] from all bodily movement and sensation he stays still. When it has illumined the whole mind, and the whole soul, it flames up again and draws the entire man out of the body and transforms him into his essential being. It is impossible, my son, for the soul who has beheld the beauty of the Supreme Good to become God while in the body.

7. T. – What do you mean by 'become God', O father?

H. – Every separate soul goes through transformations, my son.

T. – What do you mean by 'separate'?

H. – Have you not heard in the general teaching that all the souls which wander around the whole cosmos, as if separate, are from a single soul, the soul of all? Indeed there are many transformations of these souls, some more fortunate, others less. Those which are reptiles are changed[f] into aquatic creatures, aquatic creatures into those of the earth, those of the earth into fowls of the air, the air-borne into man. The human souls which gain immortality are transformed into spirits[g] and thence to the choruses of the gods. There are two choruses[h] of the gods: one is of the gods that wander and the other of those that do not move.

8. This is the most perfect glory of the soul. When the soul which has entered a human body[h] remains evil, it does not taste immortality nor partake of the Supreme Good. Being dragged away it turns back[i] on its journey to the reptiles, and that is the condemnation of the evil soul. The evil of the soul then is ignorance[j]; for the soul, knowing nothing of beings or of their nature, or of the Supreme Good, is blind and shakes with bodily pains. The evil spirit, ignorant of itself, becomes a slave to monstrous and miserable bodies. It carries its body as a burden and does not command, but is commanded. Such is the evil of the soul.

9. On the other hand, the excellence of the soul is understanding; for the man who understands is good, devoted and already godlike.

T. – What sort of man is this, O father?

H. – One who does not speak much nor gives heed to many things. He who busies himself in giving and listening to speeches, my son, is beating the air. God, Father and the Supreme Good cannot be spoken of or heard. All beings have senses because they cannot live without them, but understanding is very different from sense; for sensation arises from the objects of sense which govern men, while understanding is the fulfilment of knowledge and knowledge is the gift of God.

10. All knowledge is incorporeal, using the mind as an instrument, just as the mind uses the body. Both then come into the body, mind

and matter. All things must be composed of contrast and opposition; it cannot be otherwise.

T. – What then is this material God?

H. – The cosmos, beautiful but not good; for it is material and easily affected, and although it is first among things that change, it is second among things that are and it is incomplete. At some time it was created, and yet it always exists; it exists in creation, and it is always being created; it creates quality and quantity, and it is subject to movement. Creation is the movement of all matter.

11. The unmoving *Nous* moves matter thus: since the cosmos is a sphere, that is, a head and there is nothing material above the head, as there is nothing mental below the feet, where all is matter; so *Nous* is the head, and is itself moved as a sphere, that is, in a manner appropriate to a head. Therefore all that is united to the tissue of this head, is the soul[k] and is immortal by nature. Just as even the body is made in the soul so all that is united to the head has far more soul than body. What is further away from the tissue of the head is mortal, having within it more body than soul. Every living being, like the cosmos, is composed of matter and *Nous*.

12. The cosmos is the first; but man is the second living being after the cosmos. He is the first among creatures that die, but like other living beings he has a soul. Still, he is not only not good, but in as much as he is mortal he is corrupt. Now, the cosmos is not good in as much as it can be moved, but not corrupt as it is immortal; while man is corrupt as he both can be moved and is mortal.

13. The soul of man is carried in this way: *Nous* in the Word, the Word in the soul, the soul in the body[l]. The breath passing through veins, arteries and the blood sets[m] the living being in motion and in a manner supports it. Therefore some people think that the soul is the blood but they are mistaken about its nature. They do not realise that once the breath has to withdraw into the soul, the blood congeals, the veins and arteries become empty and then the living being is removed; and this is the death[n] of the body.

14. All things depend upon one first cause and this depends upon the One alone. The first cause is set in motion so that it again

becomes a cause. Only the One remains still and does not move. So there are these three: firstly, God, Father and the Supreme Good; secondly, the cosmos; and thirdly, man. God contains the cosmos and the cosmos man. The cosmos is the son of God, man the son of the cosmos, and as it were grandson of God.

15. God does not ignore man, he knows him fully, as God also wishes to be known. This is the only salvation for man: knowledge of God. This is the ascent to the highest abode of the gods. Thus the soul becomes wholly good; but it is not good forever, for it becomes corrupt, which happens from necessity.

T. – Why do you say that, O Trismegistus?

H. – Look at the soul of a child, my son, that has not yet accepted its own separation. Its body is not yet grown and has not fully developed. How beautiful it is to behold in every way! Not yet soiled by the experiences of the body, still virtually depending upon the soul of the cosmos. But when the body has grown large and drags the soul down to its grossness, the soul separates itself, forgets and does not partake of beauty and goodness. Forgetting becomes her corruption.

16. This also happens to those leaving the body. When the soul returns to itself, the breath withdraws into the blood and the soul into the breath; but *Nous*, being freed from covers and being godlike by nature, takes on a body of fire and ranging everywhere leaves the soul to the judgement and justice it deserves.

T. – How can you say, O father, that *Nous* is separated from the soul and the soul from the breath when you have said that the soul was the covering of *Nous* and the breath is that of the soul?

17. H. – The listener, O son, should be of one mind and soul with the speaker and his hearing should be quicker than the voice of the speaker. The formation of these covers, my son, takes place in the earthy body. *Nous* cannot be seated by itself in such a body without covering. The earthy body cannot sustain so great an immortality nor can such excellence bear contact° with a body subject to suffering. Therefore *Nous* has taken the soul as a cover and the soul, being itself divine, uses breath as fireᵖ and the breath governs living beings.

18. Whenever *Nous* is separated from its earthy body, it immediately puts on its own cloak of fire which it could not have in its earthy body, for earth cannot bear fire. It is all burnt up, even by a tiny spark. Therefore water is spread round the earth as a defence or a wall to hold off the flames of fire. *Nous* being faster than all divine thought and faster^q than all elements has fire as a body. Being the Creator of all, *Nous* uses fire as an instrument of his creative activity. The universal *Nous* creates everything, the *Nous* of man only earthly things^r. Stripped of fire *Nous* in man^s can create nothing divine, being human by reason of where it dwells.

19. The human soul, that is not every human soul, but a pious one, is spiritual and divine. When such a soul^t has freed itself from the body and passed the test of piety, which is to know God^u and to harm no man, it becomes pure *Nous*. But the impious soul remains in its own substance, restricted by itself, seeking an earthy body, that is to say a human body into which it may enter^v. No other body has room for a human soul; and it is not lawful for a human soul to fall into the body of an irrational creature. It is the law of God to protect the human soul from such an outrage.

20. T. – How then is the human soul punished, father?

H. – What greater punishment is there for the human soul than impiety? What fire makes greater flames than impiety? What savage beast mutilates the body as impiety mutilates the soul? Do you not see how many evils the ungodly soul suffers? How it calls for help and shrieks: 'I am on fire; I am ablaze. I don't know what to say or what to do. Wretch that I am, I am being consumed by the evils which possess me. I cannot see; I cannot hear!' Are they not the voices of a soul which is being punished? Or do you believe, as most do, my son, that the soul at the moment it leaves the body enters that of a beast? This is a very great error.

21. For the soul is punished in the following way. When *Nous* becomes a divine power, it is obliged to receive a fiery body to serve God; and it enters the impious soul and tortures it with the torments belonging to those that err. Afflicted by these the impious soul turns to murder, outrage and blasphemy and every kind of violence by which men affront justice. But when *Nous* enters the pious soul it leads it to the light of knowledge. Such a soul is never

insolent through sleep[w], but blesses all men, setting all things right in word and deed, since it is the image of its Father.

22. Wherefore my son, when giving thanks to God, you should pray for a mind that is noble. Then the soul can pass to a better state, not to a worse. There is a communion of souls and those of the gods communicate with those of men, those of men with creatures. The stronger take care of the weaker, gods of men and men of creatures and God of all; for He is stronger than all; and all are weaker than Him. Thus the cosmos is subject to God, man to the cosmos and the creatures to man. God is above all and around all. The powers of God are like rays, as are the natural powers of the cosmos, and the arts and sciences of men. The powers act throughout the cosmos and upon man through the rays of its nature; the powers of nature act through the elements and men through arts and sciences.

23. This is the governance of the all, depending on the nature of the One, governing through the *Nous* of the One. Nothing is more divine or effective or more able to unite men to the gods and the gods to men than this *Nous*. This is the spirit of the Supreme Good. Blessed is the soul which is wholly filled with it, wretched is the soul which is devoid[x] of it.

T. – How can you say this again, father?

H. – Do you believe, my son, that every soul has *Nous,* the Supreme Good? For that is what we speak of now, not about the servant, of which we have spoken earlier, which was sent down to punish.

24. Without *Nous* 'the soul cannot say anything or do anything'.[1] Often *Nous* leaves[y] the soul and at such a time the soul neither sees nor hears, but is like a dumb creature; such is the power of *Nous*.[z] But it leaves such a soul tied to the body and suffocated by it here below. Such a soul, my son, has no *Nous*. Therefore such a one should not be called a man; for man is a divine being and is not to be counted amongst the other creatures on earth but amongst those in heaven called gods. Indeed, if we have to speak the truth boldly, the true man is above the gods, or at least fully their equal in power.

25. Not one of the heavenly gods will leave the boundaries of

heaven and come down to earth, but man ascends to heaven and measures it and he knows the high from the low, and he understands all the other things there exactly; and even more amazing, he ascends while not leaving the earth. So great is his range. Thus one may say that man on earth is a mortal god, and that the heavenly god is an immortal man. Therefore everything is controlled[aa] by these two: man and the cosmos. But all is from the One.

*

1. Quoted from Theognis of Megara, 177-8.

Book 11
Nous to Hermes

1. N. – Mark my words and remember what I have said, Hermes Trismegistus. I shall not hesitate to speak what comes to me.

H. – Since many people have spoken much that is contradictory about the all and about God, I have not learnt the truth. O Lord, make it clear to me; for I can only trust what you have revealed.

2. N. – My son, hear about time[a], God and the all: God, eternity, the cosmos, time and generation. God creates eternity; eternity, the cosmos; the cosmos, time; and time, generation. The Supreme Good, beauty, bliss and wisdom are, as it were, the essence of God. The essence of eternity is unchanging identity; of the cosmos, order; of time, change; of generation, life and death. But the active power of God is mind and soul; that of eternity, duration and immortality; of the cosmos, the everlasting revolution of stars and planets; of time, growth and diminution; of generation, the creation of qualities. Therefore, eternity is in God, the cosmos in eternity, time in the cosmos, generation in time. Eternity stands still before God, the cosmos is moved in eternity, time passes through the cosmos and generation takes place in time.

3. The source of all is God, the essence of all is eternity, the substance of all is the cosmos; the potentiality of God is eternity, the work of eternity is the cosmos, which is never born, but is always coming into existence through eternity. Therefore it will never be destroyed, for eternity is indestructible; nor does any-

thing in the cosmos perish, as the cosmos is encompassed by eternity.

H. – What is the wisdom of God?

N. – The Supreme Good, beauty, bliss, every excellence and eternity. As eternity instills immortality and permanence into matter, it orders the cosmos.

4. For the generation of matter depends on eternity, just as eternity depends on God. Generation and time are both in heaven and earth and have two forms: in heaven they are unchangeable and incorruptible; on earth they are both changeable and corruptible. God is the soul of eternity; eternity of the cosmos; and heaven of earth. God is in *Nous*, *Nous* in the soul, soul in matter; and all these things exist through eternity. From within the soul fills this whole body, which contains all bodies, itself being filled by *Nous* and by God. From without, it contains and enlivens the whole, encompassing this vast and perfect being, the cosmos, and enlivening all creatures from within. Above, in heaven, the identity of the soul remains unchanging, but on earth it gives birth to changing forms.

5. Eternity maintains all this, whether by necessity, providence, nature or whatever anyone may suppose; and this whole is God in activity, an unsurpassable power, to which one should not compare anything human or divine. Thus, Hermes, you should never believe that anything above or below is similar to God, since then you will stray from the truth. For nothing is like that which has no like, and is alone and one. Do not believe that any of God's power is given[b] to anyone else. Who is there apart from Him, whose nature[c] is life, death and immortality? What else does He do but create? God is not idle else all would be idle, for everything is full of God. There is nothing in the cosmos, or anywhere else that is idle. For the very word 'idle' is empty with regard to the Creator and the creation.

6. Everything must always be begotten at exactly the right place. The Creator is in everything. He does not dwell just in one thing, nor does He just create in one; He begets them all. His power being active is not separate from what He has begotten, for all that is begotten exists by reason of Him. Through me behold the cosmos

open to your vision and contemplate deeply its beauty: its body without taint. Nothing is more ancient. It is ever new and ever in its prime; indeed, it exceeds its prime.

7. See how the seven worlds, arranged in an eternal order, lie beneath it, filling out eternity by their different courses. All is full of light, yet nowhere is there fire, for love and the blending of opposites and dissimilarities has given birth to light, which shines forth by the power of God, source of every good being, principle of all order, ruler of the seven worlds. See the moon, forerunner of them all, instrument of nature, transforming matter below. See the earth, set in the midst of all, fixed foundation of the beautiful cosmos, nourisher and nurse of earthly creatures. Consider the vast multitude of beings, both immortal and mortal and how between them the moon pursues her round.

8. And all beings are full of soul, and are moved by it; some around heaven, others around the earth; those on the right do not move to the left, nor do those on the left move to the right; likewise, those above do not move down nor do those below move up. And that all these things have been brought into being, most beloved Hermes, you no longer need to learn from me. For they are bodies, have a soul and are moved. These things could not merge into one without that which causes them to merge. Therefore there must be such a cause, which is one alone.

9. Since the movements are multiple and different and the bodies are not alike, yet one constant speed has been ordained for all, therefore there cannot be two or more creators. One order could not be kept by many creators. Where there are many there is jealousy of the more potent. I will explain to you: if there were another creator of changeable and mortal beings, he would have wished to create immortals, just as the creator of the immortals would wish to create mortals. But consider, since there is only one matter and one soul, if there were two creators, which of them would take charge of creation? If both, to whom would fall the greater part?

10. But understand this, that every living body consists of matter and soul, whether that body is of an immortal or a mortal being or

that of a dumb creature. For all living bodies have a soul, whereas those which are not alive, are simply matter; likewise soul, by itself, present with the Creator, is the cause of life. But He who is the cause of the immortals is the whole cause of life. How is it that He creates other living creatures from mortals? How can what is immortal and creates immortality not create what belongs to living creatures?

11. Clearly there is a Creator of these things, and it is very evident that there is only one. For soul is one, life is one, and matter is one.
   Who is He?
   Who else but the one God?
   Who else could give living creatures a soul, but the one God? Therefore God is one. It is quite ridiculous that you acknowledge the cosmos to be everlasting, the sun to be one, the moon to be one, and the divine nature to be one, yet you think God to be one of a series?

12. This one God makes everything; a plurality of gods would be absurd. Is it surprising that God creates life and soul, immortality and transformation when you yourself do so many things? For you see and speak, hear and smell, touch, walk about, think and breathe. There is not one who sees and another who hears, one who speaks and another who touches, one who smells and another who walks, one who thinks and another who breathes; there is a single one who does all these things. But none of this is possible without God. For just as if you cease doing these things you are no longer a living being, so if God ceases from these things – though it is impious to say it – He is no longer God.

13. For if it could be shown that without doing these things you cannot exist, how much more is this true of God? For if there is anything he does not create, then, disgraceful though it be to say it, He is not perfect. And since He is not idle but is perfect, He creates all things.
   Give[d] me your undivided attention for a while, O Hermes, and you will easily understand how the work of God is one, to bring all things into being, those that are, those that have once been and those that will be.

This is life, my beloved; this is beauty, this is the Supreme Good, this is God.

14. And if you want to understand this in practice, watch what happens when you desire to beget. But it is not the same with Him; for He does not experience the pleasure, since He has no partner. For working by Himself He is always in His work, for He is what He creates. If He were separated from it, all would collapse, and all would by necessity perish, because life would be no more. Since everything is alive and life is one, God is also one. If again everything is alive, both in heaven and earth, and there is one life for all which comes into existence through God, God is also that life. All then is made by God and life is the union of *Nous* and soul. Death is not the destruction of what has been put together but the dissolution of the union.

15. Eternity is the image of God; the cosmos, of eternity; the sun, of the cosmos; and man, of the sun. People call transformation death, because the body is dissolved, but in fact life withdraws into the unmanifest.

I shall tell you, as you are listening with such reverence, my beloved Hermes, that all these things that have been thus dissolved and indeed the cosmos, are transformed. Each day a part of the cosmos withdraws into the unmanifest, but the cosmos is never dissolved. This is what happens to the cosmos, these are its cycles and its mysteries. The cycles are a continual rotation and the mystery is the renewal.

16. The cosmos assumes all forms, it does not hold constant the forms that are within it but it changes them within itself. Since the cosmos is omniform, of what form would the Creator be? For He cannot be without a form. And if He is omniform He will be like the cosmos. But if He has one form, He will be inferior to the cosmos. What then shall we say of Him, if we are not to bring our discussion into difficulty? And we cannot conceive a difficulty about God. If He has any form, He has one form which is not visible and is bodiless and reveals all forms by means of bodies.

17. And don't be amazed if there is a bodiless form, for it is like the form of a word. In paintings mountain peaks appear to stand out

sharply, but they are actually smooth and flat. If you consider
what I have said, we could formulate it even more boldly and truly:
just as man cannot live without life, so God cannot live without
emanating the Supreme Good. This is, as it were, the life and
movement of God, to move all things and to make them live.

18. Some of the things being said need special attention. Understand what I am saying. All is within God; but not as if lying in a
place. For a place is not only a body, but an immovable body, and
what lies in a place has no motion. Within God everything lies in
bodiless imagination. Think of Him who contains it all. There is
nothing to limit the incorporeal, there is nothing quicker or more
powerful. It is absolutely without limit, the quickest and most
powerful of all.

19. Consider this yourself. Command your soul to go anywhere[e],
and it will be there quicker than your command. Bid it to go to the
ocean and again it is there at once, not as if it had gone from place
to place but was already there. Order it to fly up to heaven and it
will need no wings, nor will anything impede it, neither the fire of
the sun, nor the ether, nor the whirlwind, nor the other heavenly
bodies, but cutting through them all it will soar up to the last body.
And if you wish to break through all this and to contemplate what
is beyond (if there is anything beyond the cosmos), it is in your
power.

20. See what power you have and what speed! You can do all these
things and yet God cannot? Reflect on God in this way as having
all within Himself as ideas: the cosmos, Himself, the whole. If you
do not make yourself equal to God you cannot understand Him.
Like is understood by like. Grow to immeasurable size. Be free
from every body, transcend all time. Become eternity and thus you
will understand God. Suppose nothing to be impossible for yourself. Consider yourself immortal and able to understand everything: all arts, sciences and the nature of every living creature.
Become higher than all heights and lower than all depths. Sense
as one within yourself the entire creation: fire, water, the dry and
the moist. Conceive yourself to be in all places at the same time:
in earth, in the sea, in heaven; that you are not yet born, that you
are within the womb, that you are young, old, dead; that you are

beyond death. Conceive all things at once: times, places, actions, qualities and quantities; then you can understand God.

21. But if you lock up your soul in your body, abase it and say: 'I understand nothing; I can do nothing; I am afraid of the sea; I cannot reach heaven; I do not know who I was nor who I shall be.' What have you to do with God? For you cannot conceive anything beautiful or good while you are attached to the body and are evil. For the greatest evil is to ignore what belongs to God. To be able to know and to will and to hope is the straight and easy way appropriate to each that will lead to the Supreme Good. When you take that road this Good will meet you everywhere and will be experienced everywhere, even where and when you do not expect it; when awake, asleep, in a ship, on the road, by night, by day, when speaking and when silent, for there is nothing which it is not.

22. Now do you say that God is invisible? Be careful. Who is more manifest than He? He has made all things for this reason: that through them you should see Him. This is the goodness (*to agathon*) of God; this is His excellence: that He is made manifest through all. Though you cannot seeᶠ what is bodiless, *Nous* is seen in the act of contemplation, God in the act of creation. These things have been made clear to you Hermes thus far. Reflect on all other things in the same way within yourself and you will not be led astray.

Book 12
Hermes to Tat

1. H. – *Nous*, O Tat, comes from God's essence, if indeed He has essence. What sort of thing this essence is, He alone knows fully. In fact, *Nous* is not separate from God's true essence, but is, as it were, spread out from it just like the light of the sun. In men this *Nous* is God; thus some men are gods, and thenᵃ humanity is akin to divinity; in fact, *Agathos Daimon*[1] called gods immortal men, and men mortal gods. But in irrational creatures there is just nature.

2. Now wherever there is soul, there also is *Nous*; likewise, wherever there is life, there also is soul. However, in irrational creatures the soul is life devoid of *Nous*. *Nous* is the benefactor for human souls, for it moves them to the Supreme Good. In irrational creatures it works in the nature of each, whereas in men's souls it counteracts that nature. For every soul on being born in a body is immediately corrupted by both pain and pleasure. Since the body is composed of different parts, both pleasure and pain seethe within it like juices in a stew, and the soul, when it enters into these, is drowned.

3. In souls where *Nous* governs, its light is revealed, acting in opposition to all they have previously acquired. Just as a good physician causes pain by burning or cutting the body that has been gripped by disease, in the same manner *Nous* causes pain to the soul by drawing it away from pleasure, from which every disease of the soul is born.

The great disease of the soul is denial of God, next is belief in appearances, and accompanying these are all evils and nothing good. But then *Nous*, acting in opposition to the disease, secures good for the soul, just as the physician secures health for the body.

4. Human souls that are not governed by *Nous* suffer the same as the souls of irrational creatures, for *Nous* merely powers these souls and gives them up to desires. The souls are carried to desires by the force of appetite, which leads to loss of reason. Just as it is with the unreasonable nature[b] of beasts, such souls do not cease being unreasonably angered and unreasonably desirous, nor can they have enough of these evils. For anger and desires are evils without reason, without limit; and it is for these souls that God set up the law as a punishment and as a test.

5. T. – Father, then the previous teaching that you gave me about destiny risks contradiction. For if it is decreed by destiny that someone commits adultery or sacrilege or some other evil, is he who has done the deed under destiny's compulsion also punished?

H. – Everything is the work of destiny, my son, and apart from that nothing of the physical realm exists, nor do good and evil arise. It has been ordained that even the one who has done good is affected, and he acts to experience the results of his action.

6. But we are now discussing[c] evil and destiny, and we have spoken about these elsewhere. The present subject is *Nous*, its powers and variations. We have said that it is one thing in men, but another in irrational creatures. Again, in other creatures it is not beneficent. In each man, as it quells passion and desire, it acts differently and it is necessary to realise that there are some men who possess reason (*logos*) and others who do not. But all men are subject to destiny, both birth and death, for these two are the beginning and end of destiny.

7. All men suffer what has been ordained, but those with reason, who, as we have said, are led by *Nous*, do not suffer as others do; being themselves not evil, they suffer as men who have been released from evil.

T. – Again, what do you mean, father? The adulterer is not evil? The murderer and all the rest are not evil?

H. – They are, but the suffering of the one with reason will not be as an adulterer, but as if an adulterer, not as a murderer, but as if a murderer. It is impossible to escape the state of death, just as it is impossible to escape the state of birth. But for the one who has *Nous* it is possible to escape evil.

8. Let me tell you what I have always heard *Agathos Daimon* say. If he had set this forth in writing, he would have greatly helped the race of men, for he alone, my son, as the first-born god, looking down upon all things, truly spoke divine words. I once heard him say that all is one, and especially spiritual beings; that we live in power, in energy and in eternity; and that the *Nous* of this One is supremely good and also is its very soul. This being so, there is no separation among spiritual beings. Since it rules all things and is the soul of God, *Nous* is able to do just as it wills.

9. Realise this and refer this teaching to the question that you asked me earlier, I mean about destiny and *Nous*. For if you carefully lay aside captious arguments, my son, you will find that *Nous*, the soul of God, truly rules over all: destiny, law and all other things; and nothing is impossible for *Nous*, neither to raise

a human soul above destiny, nor, if the soul has been negligent, as happens, to subject it to destiny. And let this, the finest teaching that has been spoken by *Agathos Daimon* suffice for now.

T. – Father, you have spoken divinely, truly, and for the benefit of all.

10. But make this clear to me. You said that *Nous* acts as nature in irrational creatures, working[d] in their instincts. And the instincts of these creatures are, as I believe, things that change. And if *Nous* works in the instincts and instincts are things that change, is *Nous* then also subject to change, as it is associated[e] with things that change?

11. H. – Well said, my son. Your enquiry is excellent and it is right for me to answer.

All the incorporeal elements in the body, my son, are liable to change, indeed they constitute the very experience of change. Now every incorporeal element causes movement and all things that are moved are bodies, and in turn the incorporeal is moved by *Nous*. Movement is a change. Both the incorporeal and corporeal suffer change. One governs it and the other is subject to it. Release from the body is release from change; or rather, my son, nothing is free from change, all suffer it. The experience of change is different from what suffers it. The former is active and the latter passive.

Physical bodies act according to their nature; they either are still or they move. In both cases, however, there is the experience of change. The incorporeal elements are always being acted upon, so because of this they are liable to change. Now do not let these terms disturb you. For both action and experience of change are the same thing. And it does no harm to employ the more appropriate term.

12. T. – You have given the teaching most clearly, father.

H. – And see this, my son. God has endowed man beyond all mortal creatures with these two gifts: *Nous* and speech, both as much valued as immortality. Man has the spoken word. If he uses these gifts rightly, he will be no different from the immortals, and on departing from the body he will be guided by both to the realm of the gods and the blessed ones.

13. T. – But do not other creatures have speech, father?

H. – No, they make sounds, and speech differs greatly from sounds. For speech is common to all men, while each kind of creature has its own sound.

T. – But is this not true of men, father: that the speech of each nation differs?

H. – It is different, my son; but mankind is one, and therefore speech is one. Although it is translated, it is found to be the same in Egypt, Persia and Greece. You seem to me, my son, to be ignorant of the excellence and greatness of speech. For *Agathos Daimon*, that blessed god, has said that soul is in body, *Nous* in soul, and the Word in *Nous*, and that God is the Father of these.

14. The Word is an image of *Nous*, and *Nous* is an image of God; just as the body is an image of an idea, and the idea is an image of the soul. Thus the finest part of matter is air, of air, soul, of soul, *Nous*, and of *Nous*, God. And God encompasses all and is through all, and *Nous* encompasses souls, and soul, air, and air, matter. Necessity, providence and nature are instruments by which the cosmos is governed and by which matter is set in order. Now each of the spiritual beings is an essence and this essence is unchanging identity. Each body in the universe is manifold, and compound bodies, while holding this identity change into each other. Yet they always preserve that indestructible identity.

15. Furthermore, in each and every compound body there is number. For without number it is impossible for combination, composition or dissolution to occur. The One in each brings forth number and increases it, and again dissolving[f] it, receives it into itself, while matter remains one. This entire cosmos, this great god, which is an image of the greater, with whom it is united, preserves the order and will of the Father and is the abundance of life. In this cosmos, throughout the eternal cycle of ages, which issues from the Father, there is nothing, neither of the whole nor of any part, that does not live. In the cosmos not one dead thing has come to be, is, or will be. For the Father willed that as long as it exists it should be a living being. Therefore the cosmos must needs be a god also.

16. How then, my son, could there be in this god, in the image of the All, in the abundance of life, anything dead? For to die is to perish and to perish is to be destroyed. How then can a part of the imperishable perish or any part of God be destroyed?

T. – But, father, do not the creatures in Him, which are parts of Him, die?

H. – You cannot say that, my son! You are misled by terms describing that which comes into being. For the creatures do not die, but as compound bodies, they are dissolved; and dissolution is not death, but is the dissolution of a mixture. They are dissolved not to be destroyed, but that new creatures may come to be. After all, what is the activity of life? Is it not movement? What, then in the cosmos is unmoving? Nothing, my son.

17. T. – Does not the earth seem to you unmoving, father?

H. – No, my son. It is the only thing full of movement, and at the same time stationary. Would it not be absurd for the nourisher of all things, the producer and begetter of all, to be motionless? It is impossible for one who brings forth to do so without movement. It is most absurd to ask whether the fourth element earth is idle, for an unmoving body signifies nothing but idleness.

18. Then know, my son, that without exception everything in the cosmos that is, is moving, whether decreasing or increasing, and that which moves is alive. But every living creature is not necessarily always the same, for while the cosmos as a whole is unchanging, my son, all its parts are changing, but nothing can perish or be destroyed. These terms confound men, for life is not birth, but perception; and death is not change, but forgetting. Therefore all is immortal: matter, life, spirit, soul, and *Nous*, from which every living creature has been composed.

19. Now every living creature is immortal by virtue of *Nous*; man above all, for he can receive God and he shares God's essence. God communicates with this creature alone: through dreams by night and through signs by day. Through all these he foretells to man the future: through birds, entrails, inspiration, and the sacred oak. Thus man proclaims that he knows the past, present and future.

20. See this, my son, that each of the living creatures returns again and again to one part of the cosmos: aquatic creatures to the water, terrestrial creatures to the earth, and winged creatures to the air. But man makes use of all these – earth, water, air, fire – and he sees heaven, and touches even this with his mind. God is both around all and through all, he is activity and power, and so to experience God's presence is not difficult, my son.

21. If you wish to contemplate Him, behold the arrangement of the cosmos and the fine order of this array, and behold how all that is visible is so by necessity, how all that has happened and now happens is through providence. Observe matter, most full of life, this god of such magnitude, being moved with all that is good and beautiful; gods, spirits and men.

T. – But what you are describing, father, are activities.

H. – If they are just activities, my son, by whom are they set in motion? By another god? Or do you not know that just as heaven, water, earth and air are parts of the cosmos, in the same manner life, immortality, blood, necessity, providence, nature, soul, and *Nous* are His limbs; and that the permanence of all these is what is called the Supreme Good? So there is nothing that comes into being or has come into being anywhere that is not God.

22. T. – He is in matter then, father?

H. – Yes, for if matter, my son, is apart from God, then what sort of place will you give it? What do you think it could be other than a formless heap if it is not set in motion?

But as it is in motion, by whom is it set in motion? For we said that activity is an aspect of God. So by whom are all living creatures brought to life? By whom are immortals made immortal? By whom is the changing changed? Whether you speak of matter, body or essence, know that these are themselves activities of God, that the activity that is matter is His material nature, the activity that is body is His bodily nature, and the activity that is essence is His essential nature and this is God – the All.

23. And in the All there is nothing that is not. And so there is neither size, place, quality, shape nor time outside God, for He is All; and the All pervades and encompasses everything.

One of a pair of obelisks naming King Nectanebo II of the 30th Dynasty, c. 350 BC. According to the vertical inscriptions Nectanebo set up this obelisk and its fellow at the doorway to the sanctuary of the temple of Thoth at Hermopolis. During the 18th century they were moved to a position in front of one of Cairo's mosques. British Museum (Gift of King George III).

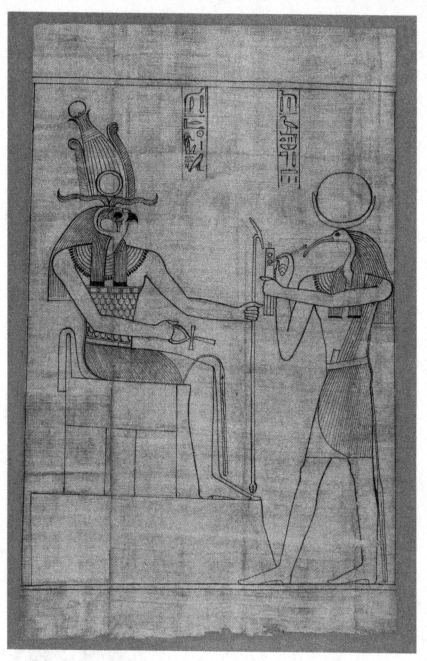

Thoth, the ibis-headed scribe of the gods, standing before the falcon-headed sun-god Re-Horakhty. Papyrus of Nestanebtasheru, 21st Dynasty, 950 BC. British Museum.

Stele with Thoth as baboon, ibis and ibis-man, 1st century AD. Allard Pierson Museum, Amsterdam.

Thoth as baboon with scroll with snake (Agathos Daimon) on his head, and as ibis, 1st century AD. Allard Pierson Museum, Amsterdam.

Alexandrian stele with snake as Agathos Daimon, 332-50 BC. Allard Pierson Museum, Amsterdam.

Bow down before this teaching, my son, and worship it. There is one way to worship God: be not evil.

*

1. For *Agathos Daimon* see Afterword, p. 79.

Book 13
Hermes to Tat

1. T. – In the general lectures, O father, you spoke in riddles about the divine nature without shedding any light. You haven't revealed anything when you say that nobody can be saved before rebirth. After you had spoken to me when we were crossing[a] the desert, I sought your help and asked to learn the teaching on rebirth, for this, above all I did not know, and you said: 'When you are ready to become a stranger to the world, I shall bestow it upon you.' I am ready now and my mind is set firmly away from the beguilement of the world. Fulfil your promise to me in which you said you would set before me either openly or in secret the way in which rebirth is bestowed. For I do not know, Trismegistus, from what sort of womb or from what kind of seed man is born.

2. H. – O son, spiritual wisdom lies in the womb of silence and the seed is truth and the Supreme Good.

T. – By whom is the seed sown, O father? I am entirely at a loss.

H. – By the will of God, O son.

T. – And what kind of man is born, O father? For he has nothing in common with me either in nature or mind.

H. – He who is born from God is of a different kind; he is a son of God and himself God, in all he is the All, composed of all powers.

T. – You speak in riddles, O father, not like father to son.

H. – This kind of knowledge is not taught, O son, but through God it is remembered, whenever He wills.

3. T. – O father, you are giving me answers which are impossible and contrived. I would like to make a frank reply to this: I have become a stranger in my father's family! Do not refuse me, father; I am your true son; tell me fully the way of rebirth.

H. – What shall I say, my son? I have only this to tell: I see within me a formless vision born by the mercy of God. I have come

out of my former self into an immortal body. I am not now what I
was before. For I have been born in *Nous*. Such a thing is not
taught, nor can it be seen by the physical body. So I have no
interest in my former physical form, for I am without colour and
cannot be touched or measured; I am a stranger to these. Now you
see me with your eyes, as something which you understand
through body and sight, but I am not now beheld with these eyes,
O son.

4. T. – O father, you have cut me to the quick, and destroyed my
faculties; for now I do not see myself.
    H. – I wish that you had now stepped out of yourself, my son,
like those who dream in sleep and yet are awake.
    T. – Tell me this also, who is the author of rebirth?
    H. – The son of God, man complete, and this by God's will.

5. T. – I am dumbstruck and bereft of my wits, O father, for I see
that your size and your features remain the same.
    H. – In this you are deceived. The mortal form changes day by
day, with the turning of time it grows and decays, its reality is a
deception.

6. T. – What then is true, Trismegistus?
    H. – The untroubled, unlimited, colourless, formless, unmoving,
naked, shining, self-knowing, the unchanging good without a
body.
    T. – O father, I am truly beside myself. I expected that through
you I would have become wise, but the powers of the mind have
been blocked.
    H. – So be it, O son. There is that which rises like fire and falls
like earth, and is moist like water and breathes like air, but how
can you perceive by means of the senses that which is neither solid
nor liquid, which cannot be grasped or released, is apprehended
only by its power and activity? This requires the ability to understand birth in God.

7. T. – I am incapable of this, O father.
    H. – May it not be so, O son; withdraw into yourself and it shall
come. Will and it is so. Make idle the senses of the body and the

spirit will be born. Cleanse yourself from the torments of the material world which arise from the lack of reason.

T. – Do I have tormentors within me, O father?

H. – More than a few, O son. In fact there are many and they are fearsome.

T. – I am not aware of them, O father.

H. – This ignorance, O son, is the first of these tormentors. The second is sorrow; the third is intemperance; the fourth lust; the fifth injustice; the sixth greed; the seventh deceit; the eighth envy; the ninth treachery; the tenth anger; the eleventh recklessness; the twelfth malice. These are twelve in number, but besides these there are many others, my son. They compel the inner man who dwells in the prison of his body to suffer through his senses. These tormentors depart one by one from the man who receives God's mercy. This constitutes the manner and teaching of rebirth.

8. For the rest, be still, O son, and keep silence; thus God's mercy for us shall not cease. Rejoice now, O son, being thoroughly cleansed by the powers of God, you are thus united with the Word. Knowledge of God has come to us, and therefore ignorance has been banished. Experience of joy has come to us, and therefore, O son, sorrow will flee to those who give place to it.

9. After joy, the power I summon is self-control; most welcome power, let us most gladly receive her too, my son; on her arrival see how she drives off intemperance. Now I call the fourth, steadfastness, the power opposed to lust. This next step, O son, is the seat of justice. See how without trial she has chased out injustice. With injustice gone we become just. I summon the sixth power, generosity, opposed to greed. With greed gone, I next summon truth, deceit flees, and truth is present. See how upon the arrival of truth the Supreme Good arises; envy has fled far from us. The Supreme Good, together with life and light, has followed upon truth, and the torments of darkness no longer fall upon us, but conquered, they all fly off with a rush of wings.

10. You know now, O son, the manner of rebirth. And with the arrival of these ten, spiritual birth is complete and it drives out the twelve, and by this birth we have become divine. Whoever, then, by God's mercy attains a divine birth is freed from the bodily

senses and is made whole by these powers[b]. He knows himself and rejoices.

11. T. – O father, I have been made steadfast through God; I now see not with the eyes, but by the operation of spiritual energy in the powers. I am in heaven, in earth, in water, in air; I am in living creatures and in plants; I am in the womb, before the womb, after the womb. I am present everywhere. But tell me again how those twelve tormentors of darkness are banished by the ten powers; how does this happen, O Trismegistus?

12. H. – This tent of the body through which we have passed, O son, is composed from the zodiac and this consists of signs[c], twelve in number; the body is of one nature and appears in every form; it exists to lead man astray. Among the signs, my son, there are pairs united in activity, as recklessness is inseparable from anger; they are indistinguishable. Under the power of right reason they withdraw, for they are banished by the ten powers. For the ten, O son, beget the soul; life and light are united, and this unity is born from spirit. In reason, the One contains the ten, the ten the One.

13. T. – O father, I see the All and I see myself in *Nous*.

    H. – This is rebirth, O son, no longer to picture oneself with regard to the three dimensional body. This is the gift of the teaching on rebirth, which I have expounded, so that we do not misrepresent the All to the many, but give it to those whom God himself wills.

14. T. – Tell me, O father, will this body which is made up of the powers, ever be subject to dissolution?

    H. – Be quiet and do not speak of the impossible; you will err and the eye of *Nous* in you will be corrupted. The visible body born of nature is far different from that of spiritual birth. For the one can be dissolved and the other cannot; the one is mortal and the other immortal. Do you not know that you have become divine and that you are a son of the One? So also am I.

15. T. – Then, O father, I wish to hear the hymn of praise which you said was there to be heard from the powers, on my[d] birth into the eighth sphere.

H. – I will recite it, O son; just as Poimandres revealed the eighth sphere to me. You do well to make haste to free yourself from the tent of the body, for you have been purified. Poimandres, the *Nous* of the Supreme, gave me no more than what has been written, being aware that I should be able to know all things by myself and to hear what I wanted to hear, and to see all, and he charged me to create works of beauty. Wherefore the powers in me sing also in all things.

T. – O father, I want to hear and to know these things.

16. H. – Be still, O son, hear the harmonious song of praise, the hymn of rebirth, which I had not thought to impart so easily, if you had not reached the very end. For this hymn is not taught but hid in silence. And so, O son, standing under the clear sky, and facing the south wind, at the setting of the sun, bow down; do likewise facing east at sunrise. Be still, O son.

Secret Hymn

17. Let every creature in the cosmos give ear to this hymn.
    Open, Earth.
    Let the rains pour without restraint.
    Trees, be not shaken.
    I am about to praise the Lord of creation, the All and the
        One.
    Open heavens; winds, be still.
    Let God's immortal sphere receive my song.

For I am about to sing praise to the Creator of all, who fixed the earth, who suspended the heavens, and who, in lands inhabited and wild, parted fresh water from the ocean for the creation and sustenance of all mankind; who ordained that fire appear for the use of gods and men. Let us give praise to Him, above the heavens, the founder of all nature.

He is the eye of *Nous*, may He receive the praise of every power within me.

18. O powers within me, sing to the One and to the All;
    with one accord, all you powers, sing praise at my bidding.

69

Divine knowledge, illumined by you, I sing through you of
the spiritual light and I rejoice in the delight of *Nous*.
Sing praise with me, all you powers.
You, Temperance, sing with me.
Justice, through me praise what is just.
Generosity, through me praise the All.
Truth, sing of the truth.
Good, praise the Good.
Life and light, from you comes the praise and to you it
returns.
I give thanks to you, Father, the strength of all my powers.
I give thanks to you, God, power of all my strength.
Your Word through me sings to you.
Receive all back through me by the Word, a spoken
sacrifice.

19. Thus cry the powers within me.
They praise the All, they accomplish your will which comes
forth from you and returns to you, being the All.
Receive an offering of speech from all beings.
O life, preserve the All within us.
O light, illuminate the All.
O God, inspire the All.
For *Nous* guides your Word, O bearer-of-the-breath-of-life,
O Creator of the world. You are God.

20. All this your man proclaims through fire, air, earth, water;
through breath, through your creatures.
From you I have discovered eternity's song of praise and in
your will I have found the rest I seek.
By your will, I have witnessed this praise being sung.

21. T. – O father, I have set this hymn in the cosmos within me.
H. – Say: In the world of *Nous*, O son.
T. – In the world of *Nous*, O father, I am full of power. By your
song and praise, *Nous* in me has been fully illumined. I, too,
strongly wish to give praise to God from my own heart.
H. – Do so with care, O son.
T. – Father, what I behold in *Nous* I speak. To you, God, first
author of generation, I, Tat, send these offerings of speech.

God, you are Father, you are Lord, you are *Nous*, receive these words of mine as you will. For by your will all things are accomplished.

H. – O son, offer an acceptable sacrifice to God, the Father of all. But also add, O son, 'through the Word'.

22. T. – I thank you, O father, for allowing me to sing as I prayed.

H. – I am glad, O son, that you have brought forth the fruit of truth, a good and immortal harvest. And now that you have learnt this from me, keep silence about this miracle and reveal to no one the tradition of rebirth, lest we be called betrayers. We have both been sufficiently careful, I in speaking, and you in listening. In *Nous* you have come to know both yourself and our Father.

Book 14
Hermes to Asclepius

1. During your absence, my son Tat wanted to learn about the nature of all things and he would allow me no delay. As he is my son and rather young and has only recently come to the understanding of these things, it was necessary for me to speak fully on each particular, so that the explanation would be easy for him to follow. Having selected the most important points we discussed, I wish to send you a summary of them, but I shall expound the more hidden meanings to you, because you are older and already understand the nature of things.

2. All manifest things have been brought to birth and are still being created, and they are not created by themselves but by another. Many things are created, indeed all manifest things, which are different from and unlike each other. Now if they are created by another then there is a maker who must be unbegotten, otherwise he would not precede all that has been created. So all that has been made was made by another; and only the one which is unbegotten can precede all that has been created.

3. Such a one is almighty, unique and truly wise in all aspects, because nothing precedes him; for he is first in number, and in magnitude; pre-eminent in transcending his creation and in creating without cease. Moreover, all that has been made, is visible, but

71

he himself is invisible. Thus he creates, so as not to be seen[a]. He is always creating, and so he is always invisible.

4. This one should understand, and having understood one should wonder and having wondered one should count oneself blessed for having come to know the Father. For what could be sweeter than a true father? Who is he? And how shall we come to know him? Is it right to give to him alone the name of God? Or that of Creator, or of Father, or of all three? He is God because of his power; Creator because of his activity and Father because of the Supreme Good. As he is that power, he transcends all created things, as he is that power in activity he comes to be all things.

Let us give up long and useless discourse. We must come to know these two: the created and the Creator; for between them there is no third.

5. In all you think and all you hear, be mindful of these two and realise these two are all; do not be perplexed about anything; what is above or below, what is divine, or subject to change, or what lies deep within; for all things are these two, the created and the Creator; but it is impossible to separate one from the other, for there cannot be a Creator without that which is created; both are in fact the same thing. Therefore one cannot be divided from the other, anymore than it can be divided from itself.

6. For if the Creator is nothing other than the creative principle, sole, unmixed, uncompounded, this principle must create by itself. As coming into being is the work[b] of the Creator, and all that has come into being cannot have come by itself, it follows that it is caused by another and that without the Creator the created could not have been born nor exist. For if either of these were without the other, it would lose its own nature, through being deprived of the other. If one accepts these two, the created and the Creator, then they are one in their union, one being first, the other following. The one who is first is God the Creator, and the created follows, whatsoever it may be.

7. And do not be wary of the full variety of creation, for fear that you will abase God and extinguish His glory. For He has only one glory, which is to create everything; this is as it were the body of

God, creation. Nothing evil or shameful can be ascribed to the Creator. These are afflictions which follow upon coming into being, like the green on copper and dirt on the body. For the coppersmith does not make the green, nor the parents the dirt on the body, nor does God create evil.

But the continued existence of creation causes evil like a kind of ulcer and therefore God brought about transformation, to cleanse the impurity of birth.

8. If one and the same painter can create heaven and gods, the earth and sea, men and all dumb creatures, and inanimate things, could not God also create these things?

To deny this shows great folly and ignorance of God! People who think this are in a most strange state. While they pretend to be holy and to worship God, in refusing to attribute to Him the creation of everything, they are not only ignorant of God, but they insult His greatness by ascribing afflictions to Him: contempt and impotence. For if He does not make all things, He does not make them either from contempt or from impotence. To think this is sacrilege.

9. For God has only one attribute, goodness (*to agathon*). And he who is good is neither contemptuous nor impotent. For God is the Supreme Good: all power to make everything. All that has been brought into being has been brought to birth by God, that is to say by the Supreme Good and by the power which can do everything. If you want to understand how He creates and how things are brought to birth, you can. Look, I will give you a most beautiful and lifelike image.

10. Behold, a farmer scatters his seed upon the earth, here wheat, there barley, elsewhere other seeds. The same man plants a vine, an apple and other trees. So God sows immortality in heaven, transformation on earth, life and movement in all. The things He sows are few and easy to count; four in all, and then there is God Himself and also generation; in these are all things which exist.

Book 16
Asclepius to King Ammon

Asclepius to King Ammon concerning: God; matter; evil; fate; the Sun; spiritual substance; divine nature; Man; the law of that which fills the universe; the seven stars; the image of man.

1. My King, I am sending you an important letter which crowns and recalls to mind all the others. It does not accord with common opinion, indeed it refutes what most people think. In fact it will appear to contradict some of the things that I have previously said.

For my teacher, Hermes, often used to say to me privately and also in the presence of Tat, that the composition of my books would appear most simple and clear to those who read them. He added, however, that they are obscure and keep the meaning of the words hidden. He said they would become even more obscure later when the Greeks decide to translate our language into theirs, which will lead to even greater distortion and obscurity.

2. When expressed in its original language, the text preserves the pure spirit of the words. For the very quality of the sound and the pronunciation of the Egyptian language carries in itself the power of what is being spoken.

Therefore, O King, as far as it is in your power, and your power is unlimited, please ensure that this text is not translated, in order that these mysteries do not reach the Greeks. For the arrogant, loose and showy style of the Greek language, will sap the majesty and strength of our own which preserves the power of the words. The Greeks, O King, use empty words which produce mere displays. That is the philosophy of the Greeks: a noise of words. We do not use such language but sounds full of power.

3. Here I shall begin my letter by invoking God, the Lord, Creator, and Father, who encompasses everything. He, being all things, is the One and being one, is all things. The totality of everything is one and is in One. There is no second here, for both are one. May you remember this principle, O King, for the rest of my letter.

For if anyone were to attack that which seems to be the All and the One, which are the same, taking the term 'All' to be separate from the One and to be a plurality, not a fullness – which is impossible – he will sever the All from the One, and thus will bring the All to naught. For of necessity all things are one, since there is in fact a One which never ceases to be one lest the totality be dissolved.

4. See how in the central parts of the earth there are many springs of water and sources of fire rising up; and in one place you can see the three natures: fire, water and earth, dependent on one single root. Hence there is believed to be a storehouse of all matter, which gives forth its own abundance and receives in return the substance from above.

5. Even so the Creator, that is to say the Sun, ever links heaven to earth, sending his substance down from above, and raising up matter from below. He draws everything around himself and into himself, and from himself gives all to all, bestowing his light in abundance. For it is he whose beneficent powers not only pervade the heavens and the air, but reach down to the lowest depth in the earth and abyss of the sea.

6. If there is a spiritual substance, then it is the body of the Sun, which his light contains. The Sun alone being near to himself in place and nature knows of what his substance is made and whence it flows. We cannot see him, but by systematic efforts we can understand him.

7. The vision of the Sun, however, does not involve effort, for the brilliance of his countenance shines throughout the entire cosmos, both above and below. Wearing the cosmos as a crown he sits at the centre. Like a skilled driver he safely guides the chariot of the cosmos binding the reins to himself, so that it does not run amok. His reins are life, soul, breath, immortality and generation. He slackens the reins so that the chariot can run freely, but not too far from himself; in fact it stays with him.

8. In this way everything is created. The Sun bestows on the immortals their everlasting life and he nourishes the eternal regions of the cosmos with the ascending light sent forth from the side that faces heaven; with the descending light that illumines

the entire hollow realm of water, earth and air, he enlivens and sets in motion birth and death.

9. The creatures in this region of the cosmos he remakes and reshapes in a cyclical movement, exchanging one for another, kind for kind, form for form. In so creating he acts just as he does with the celestial bodies. Change is constant for all bodies: for immortals without dissolution, for mortals with dissolution. Thus the immortal differs from the mortal and the mortal from the immortal.

10. Just as his light is continuous, so also he creates life continuously, without interruption everywhere, and in abundance. Around him are many choirs of spiritual powers like many different armies. They dwell together, and are not far from the immortals. Assigned to the region of men, they oversee their affairs. They carry out the commands of the gods with tempests, hurricanes, whirlwinds; with volcanoes and earthquakes, avenging impiety with famine and wars.

11. Irreverence is mankind's greatest offence against the gods; for the gods' work is to do good, men's to show reverence, and for the spiritual powers to serve. Whatever else men have the audacity to undertake through error, recklessness, compulsion (which they call destiny), or ignorance, the gods will hold them guiltless. Only irreverence comes under judgment.

12. Every kind of creature is sustained and nourished by the Sun. As the spiritual world embraces the physical and fills it out with every different kind of form, so the Sun also embraces everything in the cosmos, raising up and strengthening all generations. And when they are spent and ebbing away he receives them back.

13. The choir of spirits, or rather choirs are placed under the command of the Sun; 'choirs' because there are many different kinds of powers. They are set in formation under the stars, and are equal in number to them. Thus arrayed they serve each of the stars. Some of these powers are good and some are evil by nature, that is to say in their activity. For the essence of a spiritual power

is its activity. There are also some who are a mixture of good and evil.

14. All these spirits have been given authority over affairs upon earth and over turbulence there. They cause a variety of disorders both publicly in cities and among nations, but also in the life of individuals. For they shape our souls after themselves and arouse them by residing in our sinews, in our marrow, veins and arteries, and even in our brain, penetrating as deep as our very entrails.

15. The spirits who are set as attendants beneath each star according to what each birth merits[a], take possession of each one of us at the moment we are born and are given breath. Never stationary but turning about they change places from moment to moment. Now when these spirits enter the two parts of the soul through the body, each agitates the soul according to its own activity. But the rational part of the soul stands free of the tyranny of these powers and remains fit to receive God.

16. When by way of the Sun that rational part in a man is illumined by a ray of light (and such men are few), the spiritual powers cease to affect them. For no spirit or god has any power against one ray from the supreme God. But all other men are borne and led, both soul and body, by the powers, whose activities they dearly love. It is their thinking which is misled and misleads, not the love. Thus the powers have control over all our affairs upon earth through the instruments of our bodies. This control Hermes called destiny.

17. Thus the spiritual world depends upon God and the physical world on the spiritual, and through the spiritual and physical world the Sun receives from God a flow of consciousness, that is of creative power [*tou agathou*]. Around the Sun are the eight spheres, who depend on it; first is the sphere of the fixed stars, then the six of the planets and the one that encircles the earth. The spiritual powers depend on the spheres, and men upon the spiritual powers. Thus all things and all men are dependent upon God.

18. Wherefore the Father of all is God, the Creator is the Sun, and

the cosmos is the instrument of his creative power. His spiritual substance governs the heavens, the heavens govern the gods, and the powers, which are appointed by the gods, govern men. This is the host of gods and powers.

19. Through these instruments God by Himself creates all this, and all things partake of God; since this is so, they are God. Therefore in creating all things, he creates Himself; and He can never cease to create, for He Himself never ceases to be. As God has no end, so His handiwork has neither beginning nor end.

Book 17
Tat to a king

T. – '... if you consider it, O King, there are bodiless things in bodies.'

K. – 'Of what kind?', asked the king.

T. – 'Do the bodies which are reflected in mirrors not seem unembodied to you?'

K. – 'Certainly, Tat, what good thinking,' said the king.

T. – 'Are there not other bodiless things, for example forms which, although bodiless, appear in bodies; not only in bodies with souls but also those without?'

K. – 'You do speak well, Tat.'

T. – 'Thus the bodiless are reflected in bodies, and the bodies in the bodiless, that is to say, the physical world is reflected in the mental, and the mental in the physical. That is why you should worship the statues, because they contain the forms of the mind of the cosmos.'

Then the king, rising from his seat, said: 'The time has come for me, prophet, to look after my guests; we shall speak about the gods tomorrow.'

Afterword

The work now known as the *Corpus Hermeticum* (*CH*) consists of a collection of seventeen short philosophical treatises, composed in Greek and of varying length, some of which have not survived intact. These writings, as well as a slightly longer Latin treatise, the *Asclepius*, were believed from antiquity up to the beginning of the seventeenth century to be translations of ancient Egyptian wisdom, the teachings of 'thrice great Hermes', or Hermes Trismegistus. Hermes was the name that Greeks of the classical and Hellenistic periods gave to the Ibis-headed Egyptian god Thoth, for, simply put, they considered the latter and their own god Hermes to be one and the same. It is now generally agreed that the language of these texts points to production between the first and third centuries AD in Alexandria, a city then ruled by Rome, but culturally a cosmopolitan mix of Greek, Egyptian, Jewish and other traditions. As Gilles Quispel points out in the Preface, these texts were central to the spiritual practice of Hermetic circles in late antique Alexandria.

The teachings generally take the form of dialogues between teacher and disciple. In the first book a figure who introduces himself as 'Poimandres, the *Nous* of the Supreme', teaches Hermes. In Book 12, *Agathos Daimon*, a shadowy divinity whom the fourth-century BC Egyptian priest Manetho considered a First-Dynasty king, is also portrayed as a teacher of Hermes.[1] In most of the other books Hermes is teacher to Asclepius, a healer identified with the Egyptian Imhotep, or to his son Tat, a figure unknown outside the Hermetic writings.[2] Books 16 and 17 are the only examples of a disciple and a son of Hermes, Asclepius and Tat, acting themselves as teachers. Thus the *Corpus Hermeticum* presents three generations of the teacher-disciple relationship.

While the language of the texts reflects the diverse religious, intellectual and cultural traditions of the Alexandrian community in which they were produced, and, more specifically, of the Hermetic circles that produced them, the sources of their teachings have been the subject of considerable debate. Many modern scholars view these works as a potpourri of Hellenistic philosophical and religious speculation ascribed to an ancient Egyptian sage.[3] As Gilles Quispel notes in the Preface, others have seen connections with Egyptian tradition. Jean-Pierre Mahé's Introduction throws additional light on the *Corpus'* composition by making some very persuasive suggestions about its relationship to the aphorisms of *The Definitions of Hermes Trismegistus* and the nature of spiritual teachings in general.[4] The translators see these texts' affinities with earlier Egyptian thought as evidence of strong connections with that tradition, though their origins and lineage are admittedly impossible to pinpoint.

A brief outline of the history of the Hermetic writings and their interpretation will give a sense of the back-and-forth shifts in the efforts of clerics, philosophers and scholars to resolve the enigma of the *Corpus*.

Hermes and the Hermetic tradition from Antiquity to the Renaissance

The earliest surviving instance of Hermes' triple title comes from the Ibis shrine in Sakkara, Egypt. Records there of a meeting of the Ibis cult in 172 BC mention, both in Demotic Egyptian and Greek, the name *megistou kai megistou theou megalou Hermou*, 'the greatest and the greatest god, great Hermes'.[5] The epithet 'thrice-greatest' thus reflects the intensifying repetition of the Egyptian adjective.[6]

Thoth was the god of the moon, of writing and of learning, depicted from early Egyptian times as ibis-headed – his bill was sometimes shown as a writing implement – or as a baboon, representing intelligence. Plato lists arithmetic, geometry and astronomy among his inventions. He was also the messenger god and the conveyor of souls. In the *Phaedrus* Plato recounts how at one point Thoth had offered his invention of hieroglyphs to Thamos the god, who refused the gift on the grounds that it would debilitate the memory of his subjects.[7]

By late antiquity there was some confusion about the precise identity of Hermes. In the Egyptian tradition he was a god, but the Alexandrian Greeks considered him to be a human. In order to resolve this confusion Garth Fowden says 'at some point the Hermetists began to propagate the idea that there had been two Egyptian Hermeses, grandfather and grandson. In the *Perfect Discourse* (*Asclepius*), Hermes Trismegistus refers to the tomb of his grandfather and namesake Hermes in Hermoupolis ... Clearly the author envisages Hermes I to be identical with Thoth.'[8] Fowden goes on to outline how there emerged in the Hermetic tradition a picture of a younger Hermes, grandson of Thoth, as the translator of the Hermetic texts into Greek.[9]

It was accepted by the church fathers that the Hermes who was the author of these texts was of extreme Egyptian antiquity. In the early fifth century Augustine thought that the elder Hermes was a contemporary of Moses (fourteenth century BC).[10] The second-century BC Jewish writer Artapanus had earlier imagined that Hermes and Moses were one and the same person.[11]

When the text of the *Corpus Hermeticum* was rediscovered and translated into Latin by Marsilio Ficino, its authorship by a contemporary of Moses was taken for granted.[12] The 1481 pavement in Siena Cathedral near the main west door depicts a large image of Hermes apparently instructing men from both East and West. On the floor below Hermes are inscribed in Latin the words 'Hermes Trismegistus, the contemporary of Moses'. It was generally considered that Hermes had either instructed Moses, or been instructed by him, or both.

Thus in the Renaissance Hermes was considered to be a kind of founding father of the Judaeo-Christian tradition. But Artapanus had also written that Moses-Hermes had been the preceptor of Orpheus, the earliest of the Greek philosophers.[13] Thus Hermes came to be viewed also as the inspiration of the philosophic tradition that, according to Ficino, ran through Aglaophemus, Pythagoras and Philolaus to Plato. This view of Hermes gave the Platonic tradition almost equal authority to the tradition of the Hebrew prophets. Following the completion of his translation and commentary of Hermes, Ficino wrote 'lawful Philosophy is no different from true religion, and lawful religion exactly the same as true Philosophy'.[14] Hermes thus was a central figure in the Renaissance vision of a perennial philosophy uniting reason and faith.[15]

Modern criticism and re-evaluation

At the beginning of the seventeenth century the Egyptian credentials of the Hermetic literature were seriously undermined by the work of Isaac Casaubon. Protestant culture had never been very happy with any religious authority that was other than biblical. The Calvinist Casaubon was able to show that the Hermetic texts had been composed between the first and third centuries AD and to convince most of his contemporaries that the contents had been drawn virtually entirely from Platonic and Biblical sources.[16]

The authority of Hermes suffered a rapid eclipse. Essentially Casaubon's view of the *Hermetica* held sway in academic circles up to and including the publication of the critical text and French translation of Nock and Festugière in 1946. Indeed Walter Scott, in his 1924 edition of *The Hermetica*, went so far as to say, 'there is hardly anything of which it can be asserted without doubt that it is of native Egyptian origin.'[17] More recently Mary Lefkowitz has defended this perspective: 'its [the *Hermetica*'s] author or authors were much influenced by the very writers that Hermes the Thrice-great was supposed to have inspired, especially Plato, and his much later followers the Neoplatonists, not to mention the Hellenistic Hebrew writers known as Gnostics.'[18]

Recent work of European scholars, notably Jan Zandee, Jean-Pierre Mahé, and Gilles Quispel, lays much more stress on the contribution of Egyptian thought to the Hermetic tradition.[19] Garth Fowden's *Egyptian Hermes* has acknowledged pervasive native influence on the writings as well.[20] Again, while the Greek of the *Corpus* reflects the diverse spiritual and philosophical vocabularies of Hellenistic Alexandria, its central ideas have clear affinities with Egyptian tradition.

In some cases ideas that have been labelled Hellenistic do indeed have native Egyptian antecedents. The writings emphasise that God is unmanifest yet he appears as his own creation: 'It is plain that the One is unborn and not imagined and it is unmanifest, but it appears as all kinds of images' (*CH* 5.2). Such a view may, at first sight, appear derived from Neoplatonism, but Jan Zandee has noted that in the Egyptian tradition the sun god Ammon-Re, who is regarded in *CH* 16 as the Creator, remains hidden behind his physical appearance. A New Kingdom (second millennium BC) hymn to the sun reads, 'Thou art higher than gods and men, thou shinest before us, but we do not know thy image. Thou showest thy face, but we do not know thy real being.'[21]

The native tradition of theurgy, the magical manipulation of divine powers, is reflected not only in the so-called practical *Hermetica*, but also the *Corpus*.[22] The opening-of-the-mouth ceremony, by which Egyptian statues and mummies were 'enlivened', summoned divine powers which could then convey good or harm to the living.[23] At *Asclepius* 38a there is reference to the rites by which the gods are induced to inhabit statues and dwell among humans. A more spiritualised view of this practice is articulated at the end of *CH* 17 in advice from Tat to the king: 'Thus the bodiless are reflected in bodies, and the bodies in the bodiless, that is to say, the physical world is reflected in the mental, and the mental in the physical. That is why you should worship the statues, because they contain the forms of the mind of the cosmos.'

Garth Fowden has noted the 'authentically Egyptian' self-identification with a god that is common in the magical Hermetic texts: a devotee may summon the god, bidding him enter 'as foetuses into the wombs of women' and become identified with him so as to secure blessings and powers.[24] The *Definitions* (8.7) and the *Corpus* (5.11) speak of this identification not for securing earthly blessings, but as a spiritual transcendence.[25] This transcendence, or liberation, is also presented as the spiritual rebirth: 'Just as the body, once it has gained perfection in the womb goes out, likewise the soul, once it has gained perfection, goes out of the body... the perfection of soul is the knowledge of what is.'[26] *CH* 13, *On Rebirth*, is a dramatic account of spiritual awakening.

Jan Zandee has noted that the Greek *eis kai monos*, 'the One and Only' (*CH* 4.5 and 4.8) is the exact equivalent of the Egyptian *wc wcw*, literally, 'the Only of the only one'.[27] Egyptian sources describe the highest god as such: 'Thou (Ammon-Re) art the One, who has made everything, the absolute only One, who created all that exists.'[28] According to an ancient Egyptian cosmology the creation is the emanation of the One and Only one, who contains male and female. In the Leiden Papyrus we find 'Ammon-Re gave birth to all as a father and mother to gods and men'.[29] The same idea is expressed in the *Corpus*, where man is described as 'born from a father beyond gender' (1.15). Though Gnostic texts also speak of God as both male and female, the Leiden Papyrus provides strong evidence for a native Egyptian derivation of both the appellation and the description of the creator as beyond gender.[30]

Finally, Gilles Quispel has pointed out connections between the *Corpus* and Egyptian temple music. Books 1 and 13 contain striking hymns of praise to God sung by the disciple and teacher following spiritual enlightenment. Quispel quotes Demetrius of Alexandria (first century AD), 'When the priests of Egypt sing their hymns to praise their gods they utter the seven vowels in the prescribed order, the sound of these seven vowels is so beautiful that people prefer this music to the flute or lyre.' Quispel continues, 'The seven vowels correspond to the seven notes of the octave, which were related to the seven planets.' He later concludes that 'the esoteric songbook of the Hermetic community in Alexandria contained Egyptian hymns with Egyptian music in the Greek language'.[31] Such music plays a central role at the moments of awakening described in the *Corpus*.

A balanced view of the *Corpus* will recognize its indebtedness to the vocabulary of its milieu. One can imagine men and women of diverse backgrounds joining Hermetic associations in Alexandria. Widely read in the philosophical literature of the day – such was the collector of the fourth-century Nag Hammadi library – members of a Hermetic society would find in Plato, the Gospels, the Torah, and other works echoes that would for them and their circle confirm the universality of the ancient teaching at the heart of their programme. In turn, they might consciously make use of the language of those other traditions to attract to their group a wider following. Thus contemporary idiom and imagery were brought into the formulation of the teaching. This may have been particularly true if, as Mahé suggests, the treatises were developed as narrative settings for the aphorisms. But the contemporary idiom in no way precludes acknowledging that the teaching was fundamentally rooted in the religious tradition of Egypt.

The text and translation of the *Corpus*

Hermetic texts seem to have circulated fairly widely in the Roman Empire. They have been categorised by scholars as popular and theoretical texts, the former of which dealt mainly in subjects such as alchemy and magic while the latter, of which the most important examples are the *Corpus* and the *Asclepius*, dealt with the religious or philosophical framework into which the rest fitted.[32]

In late antiquity the text of the *Asclepius* was translated into Latin, reputedly by Apuleius. Its contents were known in Medieval and Renaissance Europe, but the Greek text from which it was translated did not survive the destruction of the Roman Empire. At least substantial elements of the *Corpus Hermeticum* were known to the church fathers Lactantius and St Augustine.[33]

However, it cannot be proved that the various treatises that now compose the *Corpus* existed as a single work in classical times. It is possible that this compilation was put together by the eleventh-century Byzantine scholar and Platonist Michael Psellus.[34] The collection did not reach Western Europe until Leonardo of Pistoia discovered a manuscript in Macedonia and delivered it to Florence, where it was translated by Marsilio Ficino.

Ficino's Greek manuscript, now in the Laurentian Library in Florence, only contains Books one to fourteen. His edition was published in 1471 and by the middle of the sixteenth century had run into two dozen editions. Other manuscripts appeared after Ficino's which contained the books that are now taken to comprise the *Corpus*. One of these manuscripts the sixteenth-century editor Adrien Turnebus used to prepare his printed edition.[35] The sixteenth-century editor Flussas added fragments from other sources as a fifteenth book, which later editors deleted. Thus the books in modern editions are numbered from one to eighteen but fifteen has continued to be omitted. By 1946 Nock was able to find twenty-eight manuscripts to consult in the preparation of his edition.

We have adhered to the enumeration of modern editors, but have included neither the fragments comprising Book 15 nor Book 18. Scott and Nock-Festugière agree in regarding the latter as not belonging to the *Corpus*.[36] It is manifestly inferior to the other books, both in content and in style (Festugière refers to it as: 'Cette insipide morceau de rhétorique').[37] No real single theme develops, but merely disconnected remarks relating to the praise of kings and of God. In addition to this there are so many gaps in the manuscripts as to render many passages unintelligible.

The *Corpus* has been translated into English a number of times.

The first translation was by Dr John Everard in 1650. The work was not then translated again until the late nineteenth century when renewed interest in ancient spiritual wisdom led to the translations of J.D. Chambers (1882), W.W. Westcott (1893-4) and G.R.S. Mead (1906). Early in the twentieth century new academic interest in ancient religion brought about the edition and translation of Walter Scott (1924-36), based on his heavily altered text. A scholarly English version was produced by Brian Copenhaver in 1992, based on the 1946 edition of Nock and Festugière. Our translation aims, as we explain in the Foreword, to provide the general reader with a new version, based on reliable texts and faithful to the spirit and beauty of the original.

Notes
(see Bibliography and Abbreviations on pp. 93-4)

1. See Copenhaver, pp. 164-5.
2. Copenhaver, p. xiii.
3. See, for example, Lefkowitz, pp. 100-4.
4. See below, *Definitions*, pp. 101ff.
5. Copenhaver, xiii-xv. Bernal, p. 139, cites a third-century appearance of the epithet at Esna.
6. Scott 1, p. 5.
7. *Phaedr.* 274Dff.
8. Fowden, p. 29.
9. Fowden, pp. 29-31.
10. *City of God* xviii, 39.
11. Eusebius, *PE* 9.27, cited in Gruen, p. 158.
12. Kristeller 1979, pp. 204-5.
13. Ficino, *Opera Omnia,* preface to the translation of *Mercurii Trismegisti Liber*, quoted by Cophenhaver, p. xlviii.
14. Ficino, *Letters* 1, p. 187.
15. Kristeller 1965, pp. 98-9.
16. See Scott 1, pp. 41-3 and Copenhaver, p. l. See also Bernal, pp. 162ff.
17. Scott 1, p. 10.
18. Lefkowitz, p. 101.
19. See Mahé 1978; 1982, Quispel, and Zandee.
20. See Fowden, ch. 1, on the durability of the Egyptian tradition in the Alexandrian religious practice, and pp. 72-4 on its relation to the Hermetic tradition in particular.
21. Papyrus Berlin 3050 VIII, 1, cited in Zandee, p. 131.
22. For the distinction between the practical and philosophical texts, see pp. 84-5, Copenhaver, pp. xxxii-xl and Fowden, ch. 3.

23. Mahé 2, 1982, pp. 97-102.

24. Fowden, pp. 28-9.

25. See below, *Definitions*, p. 115 and Introduction, pp. 104-5.

26. *Definitions* 6.2-3, adapted from Mahé.

27. Zandee, p. 126.

28. *Ammonhymn of Kairo*, Papyrus Kairo 58038 VI, 2.3, cited in Zandee, p. 126.

29. Papyrus Leiden I 344, verso II.1, cited in Zandee, p. 120.

30. For Gnostic portrayals of the creator as male and female, see *Eugnostos the Blessed*, 76, and *The Sophia of Jesus Christ*, III.4 in Robinson, p. 228. See also *The Gospel of the Egyptians*, III.42 in *NH*, p. 209.

31. Quispel 1996, p. 274.

32. See above, n. 22.

33. See Yates, pp. 6-12.

34. Scott 1, p. 29 and Copenhaver, pp. xliff.

35. Scott 1, p. 33 and Cophenhaver, p. xlix.

36. Scott 2, p. 461 and NF 2, pp. 244-5.

37. NF 2, p. 244.

Notes on the Greek Text

Book 1

a ἥδιον w/mss
b εἰδότα w/mss
c φωνὴν φωτὸς w/mss
d κτῆσιν ἐν τῷ πατρὶ w/mss
e ἐξ ὧν w/mss
f κράτος w/mss
g ἦν w/mss
h ἑαυτῷ w/mss
i ὑποκείμενα w/mss
j ἄϋπνος ἀπὸ ἀΰπνου κρατεῖται w/mss
k οὗ w/mss
l πατρὸς w/mss
m οὗ w/mss
n εὖ φημι w/mss
o παραδίδωσιν w/mss
p ὁ w/mss

Book 2

a ὁ θεός w/mss
b ὁ τόπος w/mss
c ὁ θεὸς w/mss
d αὐτῶ w/mss
e κίνησις w/mss
f στάσεώς ἐστι φορά w/mss
g αὐτὸ στρεφομένην w/mss
h περὶ αὐτὸ w/mss
i κόσμου w/mss
j omitting τῶν νοητῶν w/mss
k διόπερ ἔμψυχον τὸ καθεῦδον ἐπεὶ κινεῖ w/mss
l ἐκείνω w/mss
m εὖ φης w/mss
n from 'Nothing which is ... similar things' after mss. See NF, vol. 1 , pp. 35-6
o μέγιστα w/mss

The Corpus Hermeticum

p σώματων w/mss, omitting συνέστηκε
q λόγος w/mss
r οὗπερ w/mss
s χωρητά w/mss

Book 4

a omitting σώματι w/mss
b παντα ὑπ' αὐτοῦ w/Ferguson
c μόνω γὰρ τούτω ἀνατέθεικεν w/mss
d του ζώου w/mss
e τισὶ γὰρ ὁ φθόνος w/mss
f διαβατὸν w/mss
g 'This is the difference ... comprehends all' after mss. See NF, vol. 1, p. 53
h ἀδιαίρετον w/mss

Book 5

a ἡ φαντασία ἢ γένεσις w/mss
b κἂν w/mss
c αὐτὸς w/mss
d τί w/mss

Book 6

a ἔχουσα w/mss
b οὐδὲν w/mss

Book 8

a ἰδίου w/mss
b οὐ w/mss

Book 9

a Attributed to Hermes w/mss
b εἴπομεν w/mss
c ἀφορᾷ w/mss
d τῶ w/mss
e συσκιάσει w/mss
f omitting οὐ w/mss

Book 10

a Γενικῶν w/Patricius
b ὕπαρξις αὐτὴ w/Turnebus
c κατικνεῖσθαι w/mss
d οὕτως w/mss
e ἐπιλαθόμενος w/Hermippus
f μεταβάλλονται w/mss
g ἀνθρώπειαι ἀθανασίας ἔχουσαι εἰς δαίμονας μεταβάλλονται w/mss
h εἰς ἀνθρώπου σῶμα εἰσελθοῦα w/mss
i παλίσυρτος w/most mss
j ἐστιν ἡ ἀγνωσία w/mss
k omitting < ἐν ᾗ > NF
l σώματι w/mss
m καὶ before κινεῖ w/mss
n ὁ θάνατος w/Stobaeus
o συγχρωματιζόμενον αὐτῶ w/mss
p καθαπερεὶ πυρὶ w/Turnebus
q ὀξύτερος w/mss
r ἐπιγείων w/mss
s ἀνθρώπω w/mss
t τοιαύτη ψυχὴ w/mss
u τὸν θεὸν w/mss
v εἰς ὃ εἰσέλθη ἀνθρώπινον w/mss and Laurentianus
w ὑπνοῦσα w/mss
x κενή w/mss
y ἐξέστη w/mss
z sentence omitted w/mss
aa διοικεῖται w/mss

Book 11

a following Turnebus
b ἐγχωρεῖν w/mss
c ποιότητος w/mss
d ἐπίδος w/mss
e ἐκεῖσε w/Turnebus
f ὁρατὸν w/mss

Book 12

a αὐτοῦ w/mss
b τὸ ἄλογον w/mss
c ὁ w/mss

d συνεργεῖται w/mss
e συγχρηματίζων w/mss
f διαλυόμεναι w/mss

Book 13

a μεταβάσεως w/mss
b ἐκ τούτων συνιστάμενος w/mss
c ἐξ ἀριθμῶν w/mss
d μου w/mss

Book 14

a ἀόρατος w/mss
b ποιοῦν w/mss

Book 16

a τιμὴν w/mss

Bibliography and Abbreviations

Bernal, Martin, *Black Athena: The Afroasiastic Roots of Classical Civilization* (Rutgers 1989)

Copenhaver, Brian, *Hermetica: The Greek* Corpus Hermeticum *and the Latin* Asclepius *in a new English translation with notes and introduction* (Cambridge, England 1992)

Ficino, *Letters* 1.5 = Ficino, Marsilio, *The Letters of Marsilio Ficino,* vols. 1-5, Language Dept. of the School of Economic Science, London, trans. (London 1975-1994)

Ficino, Marsilio, *Opera Omnia Marsilii Ficini florentini insignis philosophi platonici medici atque theologi clarissimi opera omnia et quae hactenus extitere ...* (reprinted Basel 1959)

Fowden, Garth, *The Egyptian Hermes* (Princeton 1986)

Gruen, Erich S., *Heritage and Hellenism* (Berkeley 1998)

Kristeller, Paul Oskar, *Renaissance Thought and its Sources* (New York 1979)

Kristeller, Paul Oskar, *Renaissance Thought and the Arts* (Princeton 1965)

Lefkowitz, Mary, *Not Out of Africa: How Afrocentrism Became an Excuse to Teach Myth as History* (New York 1996)

Mahé, J.P., *Hermès en Haute Egypte,* vols. 1-2 (Quebec 1978; 1982)

Mahé, J.-P., 'Extraits Hermétiques inédits dans un manuscrit d'Oxford', *Revue des Etudes Grecs,* 104, 1991, 109-39.

Mahé, J.P., 'Nouveaux parallels grecs aux Définitions Hermétiques Arméniennes', *Revue des Etudes Arméniennes,* 22, 1990-91, 115-34.

NF 1-4 = Nock, A.D. and Festugière, A.J., ed. and trans., *Corpus Hermeticum,* vols. 1-4 (Paris 1946-54)

NH = Robinson, James, *The Nag Hammadi Library in English* (New York 1990)

Quispel, Gilles, ed. and trans., *The Asclepius* (Amsterdam 1996)

Scott 1-4 = Scott, Walter, *Hermetica: the ancient Greek and Latin writings which contain religious or philosophic teachings ascribed to Hermes Trismegistus,* vols. 1-4 (reprinted Boston 1985-93, 1st ed. Oxford 1924-36)

van den Broek, R. and Quispel, G., ed. and trans., *Corpus Hermeticum* (Amsterdam 1996)

The Corpus Hermeticum

Yates, Frances A., *Giordano Bruno and the Hermetic Tradition* (Chicago 1964)

Zandee, Jan, 'Hermetism and Ancient Egypt', in *De Hermetische Gnosis in de loop der eeuwen,* G. Quispel, ed. (Baarn 1994)

For an exhaustive bibliography on the *Corpus* and Hermetic studies, see Copenhaver, pp. lxii-lxxxiii.

Index

Act, Action, Active, Activity, **1**.5, 19, 22, 26; **2**.6; **3**.3; **5**.11; **8**.1; **9**.2, 3, 5, 6, 8; **10**.18, 22; **11**.2, 56, 20, 22; **12**.3, 5, 6, 10, 11, 16, 20, 22; **13**.6, 12; **14**.4; **16**.9, 13, 15, 16
Agathos Daimon, **12**.1, 8-9, 13
Ages, **1**.17; **3**.4; **12**.15
Air, **1**.5, 9, 11; **2**.11; **3**.2; **4**.1; **5**.5, 9, 11; **9**.7; **10**.7, 9; **12**.14, 20, 21; **13**.6, 11, 20; **16**.5, 8
All, the, **1**.27; **2**.17; **5**.9; **8**.2; **12**.16, 22, 23; **13**.2, 13, 17-19; **16**.3
Authority, **1**.13, 15, 32; **16**.14

Beautiful, beauty, **1**.8, 12, 14, 27; **5**.5-7; **6**.4-6; **7**.3; **9**.4, 10; **10**.4-6, 10, 15; **11**.2, 3, 6, 7, 13, 21; **12**.21; **13**.15; **14**.9
Beginning, beginningless, **1**.8-10, 17; **4**.8; **6**.1; **8**.4; **12**.6; **16**.19
Beget, begetter, begotten, **1**.13, 21; **2**.4; **5**.1; **6**.2; **8**.2, 5; **11**.6, 14; **12**.17; **13**.12
Behold, **1**.1; **5**.5; **10**.5, 15; **11**.6; **12**.21; **13**.21; **14**.10
Being
   being/beings, **2**.12, 14-15; **3**.1-2; **4**.1, 6; **5**.10; **6**.1-2; **8**.4; **9**.6-7, 9; **10**.1, 8-9; **11**.4, 7-8; **13**.19
   bring/come into, **1**.18; **3**.9; **4**.6, 10, 11; **5**.1, 8, 11; **8**.2; **9**.8; **10**.1; **11**.8, 13; **12**.16, 21; **14**.6-7, 9
   as essence, **2**.5; **6**.2; **9**.1, 5; **10**.6
   immortal/divine, **3**.1; **4**.2; **8**.1; **10**.24
   living, **1**.11, 15, 18; **4**.2; **6**.2, 5; **8**.1, 5; **9**.1; **10**.2, 11-13, 17; **11**.12; **12**.15
   mortal, **2**.8; **4**.2; **5**.6; **8**.1; **11**.9-10
   spiritual, **12**.8, 14
Birth (cf. Rebirth), **1**.9; **6**.2; **9**.3; **11**.4, 7; **12**.6-7, 18; **13**.7, 10, 14-15; **14**.2, 7, 9; **16**.8, 15
Bliss, **11**.2-3
Bodiless (cf. Incorporeal, Unembodied), **2**.4-5, 12, 15; **5**.10; **11**.16-18, 22; **13**.6; **17**
Body/bodily, **1**.1, 15, 17, 19-20, 22, 24, 30; **2**.2, 4, 8-9, 14, 15, 17; **4**.1-2, 5-

9; **5**.6, 10; **6**.3; **7**.1; **8**.1, 3-5; **9**.2, 7, 9; **10**.5-6, 8, 10-11, 13, 15-21, 24; **11**.4, 6, 8-10, 15-16, 18-21; **12**.2-3, 11-17, 22; **13**.3, 7, 10, 12-15; **14**.7; **16**.6, 9, 15-16; **17**
Born (cf. Birth), **1**.15, 19, 27-28, 4.4-5; **6**.2, 3; **9**.2, 9; **11**.20; **12**.2, 3, 8; **13**.1-3, 7, 12, 14; **14**.6; **16**.15
Breath, **1**.5, 17; **2**.8, 11-12, 14; **3**.2; **4**.1; **9**.9; **10**.13, 16-17; **13**.19-20; **16**.7, 15

Change, changeable (cf. Move), **1**.4, 24; **10**.1, 7, 10; **11**.2, 4, 9, 16; **12**.10-11, 14, 18, 22; **13**.5; **14**.5; **16**.9, 15
Corporeal, **12**.11
Cosmos (cf. Universe), **1**.8, 14-15, 19, 25-26; **2**.2-3, 6, 8; **3**.4; **4**.1-2; **6**.2, 4; **8**.1-2, 5; **9**.3-8; **10**.2, 7, 10-12, 14-15, 22, 25; **11**.2-7, 11, 15-16, 19-20; **12**.14-16, 18, 20-21; **13**.17, 21; **16**.7-9, 12, 18; **17**
Consciousness, **4**.9; **11**.13; **16**.17
Creator, **1**.9-11, 13; **4**.1-2; **5**.4, 8-9; **8**.2; **9**.5-6; **10**.3, 18; **11**.5-6, 9, 10-11, 16; **13**.17, 19; **14**.4-7; **16**.3, 5, 18
Creatures, **1**.11, 14; **6**.2; **8**.5; **10**.7, 12, 19, 22, 24; **11**.4, 7, 10-11, 20; **12**.1-2, 4, 6, 10, 12-13, 16, 18-20, 22; **13**.11, 17, 20; **14**.8-9; **16**.12

Darkness, dark, **1**.4, 6, 19-20, 23, 28; **3**.1; **7**.2; **13**.9, 11
Death, dead, **1**.18-20, 22, 28-29; **2**.17; **7**.2; **8**.3; **9**.4, 9; **10**.13; **11**.2, 5, 14-15, 20; **12**.6-7, 15-16, 18; **16**.8
Demons (cf. Divine powers, Spirits, Spiritual powers), **4**.8; **9**.3, 5
Destiny (cf. Fate), **1**.9, 15, 19; **3**.4; **12**.5-6, 9; **16**.11, 16
Devotion, devout, **1**.22; **6**.5-6; **9**.4
Disease, **12**.3
Divine, divinity, **1**.30, 2.4-5; **3**.1-2; **4**.6; **9**.1, 4; **10**.1, 17-19, 23-24; **11**.5, 11; **12**.1, 8-9; **13**.1, 10, 14, 18; **14**.5; **16**.1

95

The Definitions of Hermes Trismegistus to Asclepius

translated by

Jean-Pierre Mahé

Introduction

The Definitions of Hermes Trismegistus to Asclepius have been mainly preserved in an Armenian translation which most likely dates to the second part of the sixth century AD.[1]

Since some of the aphorisms contained in the *Definitions* seem to have been known to the author of *Poimandres* (*CH* 1),[2] we may assume that at least the main core of this collection[3] was already extant in the first century AD. Many other parallels with the *Corpus Hermeticum*, the Excerpts of Stobaeus and various hermetic fragments suggest that the *Definitions* either antedate most of the hermetic philosophical writings which have reached us or at least do not depend directly on them. The main reason why we cannot possibly assume the reverse (i.e. that a later writer has compiled the *Definitions* by picking up various sentences from the other hermetic works)[4] is that most often one and the same sentence of the *Definitions* simultaneously appears (albeit with different wording) in more than one hermetic text, which would be unlikely if each of these sentences had been borrowed separately from one particular writing.

An early date might also be assumed for our collection of aphorisms with regard to the clarity of its style and the firmness of its thought. In our edition of the Coptic and Armenian translations of hermetic writings in 1982 several clues led us to suggest that the most ancient hermetic philosophical writings were collected aphorisms such as the 'Sayings of Agathos Daimon', of which only short fragments have been preserved (cf. *CH* 10.25; 12.1.8-9).[5] Beyond *DH*, one of these collections is still extant in *SH* 11. As to the use of such collections of aphorisms we quoted *CH* 14.1 and *SH* 11.1, which depict them as summaries (*kephalaia*) of lectures delivered by Hermes and invite the disciple to reconstruct the whole teaching once he has learnt the sentences by heart (*SH* 11.3). Indeed we can easily show that many hermetic writings are made out of sentences, such as those of *DH* or *SH* 11 which are either linked up one after another with conjunctions, or commented upon or worked into a myth or a prayer.[6]

Fifteen years after this edition, we would put the emphasis not only on the mnemonic role of the sentences and their impact on the formation of hermetic philosophical literature, but more than ever on their use as spiritual exercises aimed at developing the mental faculties of the subject.[7]

Since Hermetism is not a philosophical system but a spiritual way, the main purpose of hermetic literature is not to set out theoretical teaching but to bring about spiritual progress, to raise the individual from the realm of the material bodies (including his own flesh) made out of the four elements, beyond the intelligence of this visible world, the seven planets of error and the fiery astral gods, much above the eighth or even the ninth sphere,[8] up to the supreme God, who is *Nous* and pure, endless and incorporeal light.[9]

This goal can be reached by successively developing three faculties: knowledge (*gnôsis*), reasonable speech (*logos*) and mind (*nous*).[10] Knowledge is basically a spiritual awakening and a conversion. It consists in believing that the supreme God wants to be known and can indeed be known by those who are worthy of Him. It is gained by paying heed to hermetic preaching and by living piously apart from the crowd.[11] Reasonable speech is a theoretical approach to the structure of the world and the different kinds of beings, from the supreme God down to the lowest corporeal things. It is gained by reading hermetic textbooks such as the *General Lectures* and the *Detailed Lectures* (which are no longer extant), or by following a gradual course of hermetic education.[12] *Nous* is nothing like a faculty of abstract reasoning. It is much akin to intuition or imagination. It equates to sight, inasmuch as it encompasses everything at once, even God's infinite essence. It is both spiritual light and enlightenment. It can be realised by special philosophical disciplines and essentially through mystic initiation.[13]

Now these disciplines necessarily demand the active co-operation of the disciple. The master can set out an idea or point at a direction. But the disciple will have to meditate by himself, to work on his own soul, and reveal his own *nous* by availing himself of the teaching delivered to him as a plain instrument. That cannot possibly be performed at once, but requires gradual effort,for which hermetic aphorisms can provide the most efficient guidance.

For, unlike hermetic dialogues, aphorisms do not tell a story, nor do they deal with one particular issue or set out a continuous reasoning. Quite the reverse: they purposely bear the stamp of discontinuity. While the master delivers a lecture, the disciple cannot possibly stop and meditate by himself. He must listen up to the end. That kind of teaching is appropriate for strengthening the second mental faculty, reasonable speech (*logos*). But *Nous* requires silence and meditation, which can take place in between two sentences.

Our *Definitions* adequately describe that kind of mental speech which punctuates silent meditation: 'When you keep silent, you understand; when you talk, you just talk. Since *Nous* conceives speech in silence, only that speech which comes from silence and *Nous* is salvation' (*DH* 5.1). Indeed these *Definitions* as a whole can be regarded as a general outline of hermetic spiritual exercises aimed at developing individual *nous* and making the disciple worthy of undergoing mystic initiation.

Since mind is an intuitive or contemplative faculty, the disciple who wants to strengthen his mind should first of all learn to see, or contemplate (*theasasthai, theorêsai*), God. Many exercises are designed for this purpose.[14] All of them rest on the same principle: 'Pure perception perceives the unmanifest, as it is itself also unmanifest. If you are strong enough, He will appear to the eye of *Nous*, O Tat. For the Lord appears in His bounty throughout the whole universe. Can you see pure perception and take hold of it with these hands and contemplate the image of God? But if you cannot see what is within, how can God who is himself within you appear to you through your eyes?' (*CH* 5.2).

By properly directing his mind, man can have a vision of the image of God which can be seen through the whole cosmos. In fact this image is twofold, for God 'has two images, world and man' (*Ascl.* 10). Consequently, our *Definitions* first set out the correspondence of the 'three worlds', God, man and cosmos (*DH* 1) which provides the basis for mental contemplation. Then the hermetic writer focuses on the first image, i.e. the material world (*DH* 2) which is permeated with divine presence (*DH* 3). Eventually he passes on to the second image, man, whom he first locates among the other living beings according to his mental faculties (*DH* 4). The most eminent faculty is *Nous*, which governs reasonable speech, its servant and its interpreter (*DH* 5). Thanks to *Nous* and speech, man gains the privilege of raising his eyes to heaven and overcoming his mortal condition (*DH* 6). The immortal species (being) which is in him endows him with cosmic ubiquity and vouches for his immortality (*DH* 7). Meanwhile he is submitted to natural law, but he can even in this life become a god (*DH* 8). Moreover he is the only creature who knows the supreme God. He may live in union with Him, free from fear, and carry out His Will (*DH* 9). The collection ends with a series of sentences concerning the good and evil activity of both the mortal and immortal (*DH* 10.1-6). The rest of the text is spurious.[15]

The dynamic of contemplation normally requires that we do not dwell on the visible things but rather pass on to the inner world. We do not need a concrete vision, focussed on appearance and material details, but a spiritual one, where imagination tries to apprehend the invisible beyond the corporeal. This may be easier when we reach to our innermost experience. But hermetism has worked out a method which enables us to go much further by transcending the limit that we always set between us and the others, inside and outside, present, past and future, our individual being and the immensity of the universe.

This method which is called 'becoming *Aiôn*' (eternal), is most vividly described in *CH* 11.19-21 and 13.11; but our *Definitions* clearly contain quite a range of sentences which may help the reader get rid of the limits of common consciousness by constantly transcending concrete existence through comparisons or analogies, which start with most trivial experiences ('just as ...') and end in spiritual insights into mystic belief ('likewise ...').

Thus we are encouraged to experiment with the wonderful mobility of human beings who, thanks to their threefold essence – intelligible, animated and material (*DH* 6.1) – are not confined to one part of the universe (e.g. like fishes in the sea or gods in heaven), but are 'at once in earth, in the sea, and in heaven' (*CH* 11.20). Not only can humankind push away the barriers of space but they also can escape the bondage of time by picturing to themselves the dawn of existence in the womb, or even soul before entering the body and after leaving it (*DH* 6.2-3; 7.3-4). This kind of meditation is nothing like mere fancy. On the contrary it is a way of seeing the invisible, of anticipating the Great Beyond, a real training for immortality.

Indeed becoming immortal is just a matter of will: 'You can even become a god if you want, for it is possible. Therefore want and understand and believe and love: then you have become it !' (*DH* 8.7).

Seldom if ever have the basic intuitions of hermetism been expressed with such a concentrated strength. The *Definitions* are perhaps at once the plainest and the deepest of all hermetic writings. We can read it as a mere résumé of elementary teaching. Most of the hermetic dialogues take up the same sentences and comment upon them at the *logos*-level, which is but the second stage of the way to immortality. Rarely do they go one step further and reveal to us the spiritual meaning of the text.

It is no surprise that at least one sentence of this collection also occurs in the *Gospel of Thomas*. Both texts comprise sacred sayings and secret teachings meant to strike imagination and to strongly impress their reader. Moreover we could venture to assert that, in regard to the other hermetic writings, the *Definitions* are almost in the same position as the *Gospel of Thomas* with regard to the four Gospels. In both cases, we have the aphorisms by themselves on the one hand, and sayings worked into a reasoned account or narrative on the other. The problem is whether the story is missing because it does not yet exist (or it is unknown to the compiler) or quite on the contrary, because it has been purposefully ruled out.

We can also assert the comparison for essential reasons. Just as some gnostic writer may have thought that the earthly life or even the human and ethnic identity of Jesus, the Living One, was a mere accident or maybe an illusion, whereas his words conveyed eternal truth and universal salvation, so that their purity must be preserved, wrapped up in silence (instead of being swamped by a mass of irrelevant details, such as to know whether this word has been uttered in Jerusalem or in Capernaum, etc.), likewise the hermetic author of our text seems to have deliberately eliminated all kind of commentary in order to free his readers from the heaviness of abstract reasoning, to raise them above space and time and to hand over to them the very essence of meditation. You do not easily forget such a text. Hermetic sentences get mysteriously carved in your memory. They are still at work on your mind even when you do not think of them. For 'it dwells in those who have already seen it and draws them upward, just as they say a magnet draws up iron' (*CH* 4.11).

The Definitions

*

The Armenian version of the *Definitions* was first published by H. Manandyan in 1956, on the basis of six manuscripts of Yerevan, along with a Russian translation by S. Arevšatyan.[16] In 1976 we translated Manandyan's text into French and we provided our translation with numerous parallels drawn from the other hermetic writings.[17] Somehow later during the same year, quite independently from ours, appeared another French translation by G.-M. De Durand.[18]

Eventually we had access to other Armenian manuscripts kept in Venice, Vienna, Jerusalem and Yerevan. We also discovered that *DH* 10.7 was identical to *SH* 19.1 and *DH* 11 was nothing but an abridged rewriting of the Armenian version of Nemesius, ch. 5.[19] Moreover we tried to compare the Armenian with other collections and we raised the question of the Egyptian background. Therefore we prepared a new critical text, along with a revised translation and commentary which was included in 1982 in our edition of new hermetic documents.[20]

Sometime in 1988 J. Paramelle discovered excerpts from the Greek original of the text in the codex Clarkianus 11 of the Bodleian Library in Oxford. The same codex also contained other hermetic excerpts including some fragment of a thus far unknown treatise *On Soul*. All of these materials were edited in 1991.[21]

The purpose of the present translation is very modest. It just aims at putting together all of these textual data. The italicised paragraphs represent the Greek excerpts as we have reconstructed them. In these passages we did not deem it necessary to bracket such short segments which are preserved only in Armenian, since the reconstruction is virtually certain. For this and other critical issues, we simply refer to the 1991 edition. The commentary is quite succinct. Except for some philosophical remarks, it is a mere list of references to the most obvious hermetic parallels to the text.

Notes

1. The first Armenian writers who quote this translation are the historian Eliše Vardapet who can be placed 'in the last decade of the sixth century or later' (Thomson 1982, p. 27); the anonymous *Yačaxapatum*, a collection of homilies whose date is not precisely known, although inter-

nal evidence also points to the sixth century; and Anania Širakac'i who wrote his *K'nnikon* (Quadrivium) between 661 and 667 AD (cf. *HHE*, vol. 2, p. 336 s.). Paramelle-Mahé (1990-91), pp. 115-17 (nn. 2 and 7a).

The Armenian version belongs to the so-called 'Hellenising school' whose activities seem to have taken place from the early sixth century to the early eighth (*HHE*, vol. 2, pp. 327-8). Terian's hypothesis (Terian 1982, p. 183) i.e. 570-3, accepted by Fowden 1986, p. 10, without any discussion, seems too late.

2. Compare e.g. *DH* 1.4 'God is *Nous*' with *CH* 1.6; *DH* 6.3 'the perfection of soul is the knowledge of the beings' with *CH* 1.3; *DH* 7.3 'soul enters the body from the light to darkness' with *CH* 1.20; *DH* 8.4 'Every man has got a body and a soul but not every soul has got *Nous*' with *CH* 1.22; *DH* 9.2 '*Nous* is light and light is *Nous*' with *CH* 1.17; *DH* 9.4 'Whoever thinks of himself in *Nous* knows himself and whoever knows himself knows the whole' with *CH* 1.18. This last parallel was first commented upon by G. Quispel in a paper read in Quebec-City in 1978 (Quispel 1981, p. 260). A similar sentence can also be found in the *Gospel of Thomas* (Nag Hammadi Codex II, 51, 9-10) and in the *Book of Thomas the Athlete* (ibid. 138, 17ff). Camplani (1993, p. 420) adduces other parallels (including Plato, *Alcibiades Major* 130E) and observes that nothing prevents us from assuming as well that *CH* 1 and *DH* might have known the sentence independently from each other. That would be indeed most likely, if there were no other parallels between the two writings. It would take too long to discuss here in minute detail the date of *Poimandres* (*CH* 1). Despite contrary opinions in recent works, we cannot see any cogent reason for placing this writing much later than AD 115.

3. Collections of aphorisms normally are liable to additions and interpolations. Thus we might suspect that *DH* 10.7 is a later addition, as Dörrie (1957, p. 446) had already assumed. Indeed that paragraph is identical to *SH* 19.1, which, in turn, is much akin to *SH* 15-22. These excerpts clearly bear the stamp of the so-called 'pneumatic' medical school witnessed by the *Medical Definitions* of Ps.-Galianus, which cannot have been extant before the third century AD (NF, vol. 3, p. cxiii, *HHE*, vol. 2, p. 329). In addition, we might object that some sentences of *DH* 2 (concerning the elements) or of *DH* 10 are also close to *SH* 15-19. As to *DH* 11 see below, n. 20.

4. This seems to be what Fowden (1986, p. 10) assumes, when he writes that 'the *Definitions* offer an interesting parallel to the dismemberment of the *Perfect Discourse* during the prehistory of Nag Hammadi Codex VI'.

5. *HHE*, vol. 2, pp. 310-12. In 1982, the Demotic *Book of Thoth* – a prehermetic dialogue discovered in 1993 by K.Th. Zauzich and Richard Jasnow – was still unknown. It is noteworthy that this work contains a short collection of Thoth's precepts entitled *The Little Book of Advice*. Although none of those precepts are directly echoed by any Greek hermetic aphorism, it may confirm our assumption (which has been sharply criticised by G. Fowden 1986, pp. 71-2) that Greek hermetic philosophical literature is closely connected with Greek hermetic gnomologies which in turn bear the influence of Egyptian Wisdoms or instructions (Mahé 1996, pp. 358-9).

6. *HHE*, vol. 2, pp. 408-36.

7. As to the notion of 'spiritual exercises', we mainly refer to Hadot 1991.

8. This is the purpose of the initiation described in *Ogd.* (cf. *HHE*, vol. 1, pp. 62-87).

9. On the hermetic way, see Mahé 1991a.

10. Mentioned in the reverse order (*nous, logos, gnôsis*), i.e. from top to bottom, in *NH* VI, 63,33-64,19 (cf. Mahé 1991a, p. 350).

11. Mahé 1991a, pp. 350-5.

12. Ibid., pp. 355-61.

13. Ibid., pp. 361-6. See above, n. 8.

14. The main texts (*CH* 10.6; 11.14; 12.21; 14.9-10) are commented upon in *HHE*, vol. 2, pp. 209-10.

15. Cf. above, n. 3 and below, n. 19.

16. Manandyan-Arevšatyan 1956.

17. Mahé 1976.

18. De Durand 1976.

19. *HHE*, vol. 2, pp. 331-2.

20. *HHE*, vol. 2, pp. 273-406.

21. Paramelle-Mahé 1990-91 and 1991. In the latter (p. 123) we have discussed whether *HO* (which displays many similarities with *SH* 8, 15-20 whereas *SH* 19.1 is quoted in *DH* 10.7) has any literary connection with *DH*. In fact in the manuscript Clarkianus 11, the excerpts from *DH* are separated from *HO* with a short quotation of *CH* 16.4. Moreover, although *HO* also includes some definitions, its contents as a whole sounds more like a continuous reasoning than like aphorisms. Therefore if any connection has ever existed between the two texts, it can be only secondary and accidental.

From Hermes Trismegistus to
Asclepius: Definitions

1

1. God: an intelligible world;[1] world: a sensible God; man: a destructible world; God: an immovable world; heaven: a movable world; man: a reasonable world.[2] Then there are three worlds.[3] Now the immovable world (is) God, and the reasonable world is man: for both of (these) units (are) one: God and man after the species.[4]

2. Consequently (there are) three worlds on the whole: two units (make up) the sensible and one (is) the intelligible; one (is) after the species, and the third one (is) after (its) fullness.[5] All of the multiple (belongs to) the three worlds; two of them (are) visible: (namely) the sensible and man, (that) destructible world; and the intelligible is this God:[6] he is not visible, but evident within the visible (things).[7]

3. Just as soul keeps up the figure[8] (while being) within the body, which cannot possibly be constituted without a soul, likewise all of that visible cannot possibly be constituted without the invisible.[9]

4. Now man is a small world[10] because of soul and breath, and a perfect world whose magnitude does not exceed the sensible god, (i.e.) the world. The world (is) intelligible and God (is) Nous;[11] (he is) the truly uncreated, the intelligible; by essence, the uncreated and the ineffable, the intelligible[12] good. In a word, God is the intelligible world, the immovable Monad, the invisible world, the intelligible, invisible and ineffable[13] good.[14]

5. God is eternal and uncreated; man is mortal (although) he is ever-living.[15]

2

1. Nous is the invisible good;[16] soul (is) a necessary movement adjusted to every (kind of) body.[17] A body is (made out) of the four qualities,[18] (as) a well-tempered composition[19] of warm, cold, dry and wet: of warm (i.e.) of fire, of cold (i.e.) of air, of dry (i.e.) of earth, of wet (i.e.) of water.[20] Breath is the body of soul[21] or the column of soul.[22]

2. Heaven is an eternal body, an immutable body, unalterable and mixed up out of soul and Nous.[23] Air is the separation of heaven from the earth or the conjunction of heaven with earth.[24] What is air? They call 'air' the interval between heaven and earth,[25] by which they are not separated from each other, since heavens and earth are united (with each other) by the air.

3. Earth is the support of the world, the basis of the elements, the nurse of the living (beings), the receptacle of the dead;[26] for (it comes) last[27] after fire and water, since it became what (it is) after fire and water.[28] What is the power of the world? To keep up for ever the immortal (beings), such as they came into being, and to always change the mortal.[29]

4. Water is a fecund essence,[30] the support of earth,[31] as a nutritive essence.

5. Fire is a sterile essence, the duration of the immortal bodies and the destruction of the mortal: an infertile substance, in as much (it belongs to) the destructive fire which makes (things) disappear; and the perpetuation[32] of the immortal (beings), since what cannot be consumed by fire is immortal and indestructible, but the mortal can be destroyed by fire.

6. Light is a good, a clear vision,[33] (which makes) appear all of the visible (things). The essence of fire is burning. However, fire is one (thing) and light is another one.[34] For what fire has reached shall be destroyed, but light appears just as it is by itself. Every move of soul is perceived by Nous; since it is some (kind of) energy, breath performs (it).[35]

3

1. Nothing is uninhabited by God,[36] for where heaven is, God (is) too,[37] and where the world is, heaven (is) too. I think[36a] that God is in heaven, and heaven in the world.

2. Many (places) are uninhabited by humans; for where the world is, the earth (is) too,[38] but man is not on every earth. The sea is large as well as the earth, but heaven by itself (is as much as) both the sea and the earth. [And he wanted to say that, by its magnitude, heaven is (as much as) both the earth and the sea, so large as the two of them may be, since by taking everything into (itself), it encompassed it and it contains it enclosed within (itself).[39]]

3. Heaven is larger than everything, and the sun than earth and sea, for it extends beyond both of them. However the earth is larger than the sea, because the sea (comes) from it. And in heaven are all (the beings), for it contains the superior ones and it (also) contains the inferior, enclosing them from every side.

4. God is the good (which is) previous to all the intelligible (beings); God is the father of the intelligible;[40] heaven is the maker of the body.[41] The magnitude of the light of the sun is earth and sea;[42] the magnitude of heaven (is) the world; the magnitude of the world is God.

4

1. The living (beings) in heaven are constituted of fire and air,[43] and those (which are) on earth of the four elements.[44] Man (is) a reasonable living (being),[45] for he has Nous;[46] but all of the other living (beings) which are endowed with voice[47] have breath and soul, since *all that decreases and increases is a living (being).*[48]

2. *And among the living (beings), some are immortal and animated,*[49] *some have Nous, soul and spirit, some (have) only spirit, some (have) soul and spirit, and others only life.*[50] *For life can acquire consistency without spirit, Nous, soul and immortality, but all of the others without life cannot possibly exist.*[51]

5

1. *(Reasonable) speech*[52] *is the servant of Nous.*[53] *For what Nous wants, speech in turn interprets.*[54] Nous sees everything,[55] and eyes all corporeal (things).[56] And yet Nous does not become an observer for the eyes, but the eyes for Nous.

2. To Nous nothing is incomprehensible,[57] to speech nothing ineffable:[58] when you keep silent, you understand;[59] when you talk, you (just) talk. Since Nous conceives speech in silence,[60] only (that) speech (which comes) from silence and Nous (is) salvation.[61] (But that) speech (which comes) from speech (is) only perdition; for by (his) body man is mortal, but by speech (he is) immortal.[62]

3. Who does not understand speech has no Nous, who talks without Nous says nothing:[63] since he understands nothing, he has no Nous and he talks, for his talk is a crowd and a crowd has neither Nous nor (reasonable) speech.[64] Speech endowed with Nous is a gift of God;[65] speech without Nous is a finding of man.[66] Nobody sees heaven and what (is) therein, but only man.[67] Only man has Nous and speech.[68]

6

1. Just as the gods are God's possession, (so is) man too; and man's possession is the world:[69] if there were nobody to see (it), what would be seen would not even exist.[70] Only man understands the intelligible (things) and sees the visible, for they are no aliens to him.[71] *Man has at once the two natures, the mortal and the immortal (one).*[72] *Man has the three essences, (namely) the intelligible, the animated and the material (one).*[73]

2. *Just as you went out of the womb, likewise you will go out of this body; just as you will no longer enter the womb,*[74] *likewise you will no longer enter this material body. Just as, while being in the womb, you did not know the (things which are) in the world, likewise when you are outside the body, you will not know the beings (that are) outside the body. Just as when you have gone out of the womb, you do not remember the (things which are) in the*

womb, likewise, when you have gone out of the body, you will be still more excellent.[75]

3. *The present (things) follow close upon the past, and the future (close upon) the present.*[76] *Just as the body, once it has gained perfection in the womb, goes out,*[77] *likewise the soul, once it has gained perfection, goes out of the body. For just as a body, if it goes out of the womb (while it is still) imperfect can neither be fed nor grow up, likewise if soul goes out of the body without having gained perfection it is imperfect and lacks a body; but the perfection of soul is the knowledge of the beings.*[78] *Just as you will behave towards your soul when (it is) in this body, likewise it will behave towards you*[79] *when it has gone out of the body.*

– Contain yourself,[80] O Trismegistus!

7

1. But now, what is man? What (else) if neither body nor soul?[81]

– Aye, dear Asclepius, who (ever) is not soul, is neither Nous nor body. For (one) thing is what becomes the body of man, and (another) thing what comes in addition to man. Then, what should be called truly a man,[82] O Asclepius, and what is man? The immortal species[83] of every man.

2. *And <the species> of every living (being) <is (only) in one part of the world,> but the sole species of man (is) at once in heaven, on earth, in the water and in the air.*[84] *Just as the body is marvellously moulded in the womb,*[85] *likewise the soul in the body.*

3. *From the murk into light the body goes out of the womb, but soul enters the body from the light into darkness.*[86] *The sight of the body is the eye; but that of soul is Nous. Just as a body which has (got) no eyes sees nothing, likewise a soul which has (got) no Nous is blind.*[87] *Whatever the (babe) in the womb will crave for, so will the pregnant woman desire the same; likewise whatever (Nous) in soul will crave for, so will man desire the same.*

4. *Soul enters the body by necessity,*[88] *Nous (enters) soul*[89] *by judgement.*[90] *While being outside the body, soul (has) neither quality nor quantity;*[91] *(once it is) in the body it receives, as an*

accident,[92] quality and quantity as well as good and evil: for matter brings about such (things).[93]

5. God is within himself, the world is in God, and man in the world.[94] His (i.e. man's) deficiency is ignorance, his plenitude is the knowledge of God.[95] [**✕** He says that evil (consists) in ignorance and good in knowledge **Ω**.[96]]

8

1. All (beings) cannot possibly exceed their own capacity.[97] Nature is everyone of the beings of this (world);[98] there is a law which is in heaven above destiny, and there is a destiny which has come into being according to a just necessity; there is a law which has come into being according to the necessity of humans, there is a god who has come into being according to human opinion.[99]

2. Divine bodies do not have access paths for sensations, for they have sensations within themselves, and (what is more) they are themselves their own sensations.[100] What God does, man does not do it; and whatever God does, he does it for man; but what man does, he does it for soul.[101]

3. Those who worship idols (worship plain) pictures. For if they worshipped with knowledge, they would not have gone astray, but since they do not know how they should worship, they have gone astray, (far) from piety.[102] Man has the faculty of killing,[103] God of giving life.

4. *The body increases and reaches perfection*[104] *due to nature; and soul fills up with Nous.*[105] *Every man has a body and a soul, but not every soul has Nous.*[106] *Consequently there are two (types of) Nous: the one (is) divine*[107] *and the other (belongs to) soul. Nevertheless there are certain men who do not have even that of soul.*[108] Who(ever) understands the body, also understands soul; who(ever) understands soul, also (understands) Nous, because the admirable is (a) natural (object) of contemplation: each of the two is seen by means of the other.

5. Nature is the mirror of truth;[110] the latter is at once the body of

the incorporeal (things)[111] and the light of the invisible.[112] The generous nature of this (world) teaches all (the beings).[113] If it seems to you that nothing is a vain work, you will find the work and the craftsman,[114] if it seems to you (like) a mockery, you will be mocked at.[115]

6. You have the power of getting free since you have been given everything.[116] Nobody envies you.[117] Everything came into being for you, so that by means of either one (being) or of the whole, you may understand the craftsman.[118] For you have the power[119] of not understanding with your (own) will; you have the power of lacking faith and being misled, so that you understand the contrary of the (real) beings. Man has as much power as the gods. Only man (is) a free living (being), only he has the power of good and evil.

7. You do not have the power of becoming immortal ; neither does, indeed, the immortal (have the power) of dying.[120] You can even become a god if you want, for it is possible.[121] *Therefore want and understand and believe and love: then you have become (it)!*[122]

9

1. *Every man has a notion of God: for if he is a man, he also knows God. Every man, by the very (fact) that he has (got) a notion of God, is a man,*[123] *for it is not (given) to every man to have (such a) notion. Man and the gods and all things (exist) by God and because of man. God is everything*[124] *and there is nothing outside God, even that which does not exist: since as to God, there is no such thing, even one single <that he is not himself>.*[125] *Man (comes) from another man, the gods (exist) because of God.*[126] *Man (exists) because of God; everything because of man.*[127] *God rules over man; man over the whole.*[128]

2. *The exterior (things) are understood by the external (organs): the eye sees the exterior (things), and Nous the interior.*[129] *The exterior (things) would not exist, if there were not the interior (ones).*[130] *Wher(ever) Nous (is), there is light; for Nous is light and light (is) Nous.*[131] *Who(ever) has Nous is enlightened,*[132] *and who(ever) has not Nous is deprived of light.*

3. *Who(ever) knows God, does not fear God;*[133] *who(ever) does not know God fears God. Who(ever) knows none of the beings fears everyone; who(ever) knows all of them fears none.*[134]

4. Soul's illness: sadness and joy;[135] soul's passions: desire and opinion.[136] Bodies are similar to souls when they are seen: none (is) ugly (if it is) good, none is evil (if it is) honest. Everything is visible to one who has Nous; who(ever) thinks of himself in Nous knows himself and who(ever) knows himself knows everything.[137] Everything is within man.

5. *Who(ever) behaves well towards his body, behaves badly towards himself.*[138] *Just as the body, without a soul, is a corpse, likewise soul, without Nous, is inert.* Once a soul has entered the body, it (soul) will acquire Nous.[139] That which does not acquire (it), goes out such as it had entered. For every soul, before entering the body, is deprived of Nous; then Nous joins it from the body, so that eventually the soul becomes endowed with Nous.[140] That (soul) which has gone out of the human body has (got) an ill memory: for soul, (even) covered with the body, is forced to remember its (soul's) unforgetfulness. One change is unforgetful and (another) change brings about forgetfulness.

6. Wher(ever) man is, also (is) God. God does not appear to anybody but man.[141] Because of man God changes and turns into the form of man.[142] God is man-loving and man is God-loving. There is an affinity between God and man. God listens only to man, and man to God.[143] God is worthy of worship, man is worthy of admiration.[144] God does not appear without man; man is desirable to God and God to man, because desire comes from nowhere, but from man and God.

7. Humans work the land,[145] (and) stars adorn heaven.[146] The gods have heaven; humans, <heaven>,[147] earth and sea; but the air is common to gods and humans.

10

1. What is good? What bears no comparison.[148] Good is invisible,[149]

(but) evil is conspicuous.[150] What is a female? A receptive fluidity.[151] What is a male? A seminal fluidity.

2. Nature in man is omniform,[152] and (it is) an energy[153] endowed with all qualities (whose) force (is) invisible and effects (are) conspicuous. An energy is a movement.[154] Matter is a wet essence;[155] a body is a agglomoration of matter.[156]

3. Nous (is) in soul, and nature (is) in the body. Nous (is) the maker of soul, and soul, (the maker) of the body.[157] Nous (is) not in all soul,[158] but nature (is) in all body.[159]

4. The immortal nature (is) the movement of the mortal nature,[160] (as to) mortality, earth is its grave; (and) heaven (is) the place of the immortal.[161] The immortal came into being because of the mortal, but the mortal comes into being by means of the immortal.[162] Evil is a deficiency of good,[163] good (is) fullness of itself.[164]

5. Soul is bound to be born in this world, but Nous is superior to the world.[165] Just as Nous is unbegotten, so is matter too, (although) it (can be) divided. Nous is unbegotten, and matter (is) divisible; soul is threefold,[166] and matter has three parts;[167] generation[168] (is) in soul and matter, (but) Nous (is) in God for the generation of the immortal (beings).

6. Providence and Necessity[169] (are), in the mortal, birth and death,[170] and in God, unbegotten (essence). The immortal (beings) agree with one another and the mortal envy one another with jealousy,[171] because evil envy arises due to knowing death in advance. The immortal does what he always does, but the mortal does what he has never done. Death, if understood, is immortality;[172] if not understood (it is) death. They assume that the mortal (beings) of this (world) have fallen under (the dominion) of the immortal, but (in reality) the immortal are servants of the mortal of this (world).[173]

[7. *Therefore soul is an immortal essence,[174] eternal, intellective, having, as an intellectual (thought), its reason endowed with Nous. By understanding nature, it attracts[175] to itself the intellect of (the planetary) harmony;[176] then, once it is freed from this natural body, it remains alone with itself (and) is grieved, belonging only to itself in the intelligible world. It rules on its reason.*[177]]

Notes
(see Bibliography and Abbreviations on p. 123)

1. *CH* 8.1; *Ascl.* 8,0.
2. *CH* 11.2; cf. *CH* 2.8; 10.11; *SH* 11.2,48.
3. *CH* 10.14; *SH* 11.2,6; cf. *CH* 8.
4. *tesak* = *eidea* / *idea* in *DH* 8,1 may be the 'essential' part of man.
5. The world is full, cf. *Ascl.* 33. In other contexts God is fullness, cf. *CH* 16.3; *Ascl.* 26; *CH* 6.1,4.
6. i.e. the visible world.
7. *CH* 5.1; 14.3.
8. *tesak* literally 'species', cf. *DH* 1.1.
9. *CH* 5.1.
10. i.e. a microcosm, cf. Firmicus Maternus, *Mathesis* III, proem. 2-4; Olympiodorus (Berthelot-Ruelle, p. 100, line 18ff.); *Iatromathematica* (Ideler 1841, p. 387).
11. *CH* 1.6.
12. *CH* 2.12.
13. *CH* 1.31.
14. *CH* 11.2; 2.14-16; 6.
15. Cf. *NH* 6.67,29-30; *aeizôos* normally applies to the world (*CH* 4.2; 8.2).
16. *CH* 4.9, and *DH* 10.1.
17. *SH* 3.4; *CH* 12.1.
18. *CH* 2.11; *Ascl.* 7; cf. *SH* 2A.2; 24.9; 26.14.
19. *SH* 16.3; 26.8.
20. Cf. *SH* 24.9; 26.13-30.
21. *SH* 26.29.
22. Cf. *SH* 15.7.
23. *CH* 11.4; *SH* 11.2,43.
24. *CH* 5.5.
25. *SH* 25.11.
26. *CH* 11.7; *Ascl.* 2; *SH* 11.2,42; cf. *CH* 12.17.
27. *SH* 11.2,45.
28. *SH* 15.2.
29. Cf. *CH* 16.8; *CH* 12.22; 8.4.
30. *FH* 27.
31. *FH* 32; *SH* 15.2; *CH* 1.5; 3.1-2.
32. *yarut'iwn* = *diamonē*, as in the old Armenian version of Philo.
33. *CH* 10.4.
34. *CH* 11.7.

35. *SH* 19.7.

36. *CH* 5.10.

36a. The following is perhaps a gloss of the compiler; see n. 39.

37. Some manuscripts add: 'and where is the world, God (is) too'.

38. Or 'heaven (is) too' according to some manuscripts.

39. Likely a gloss of the compiler (see *DH* 7.5).

40. *CH* 2.5,16.

41. *CH* 6.2.

42. *CH* 16.8; cf. *FH* 32.

43. *SH* 26.30.

44. *SH* 2A.1-2.

45. *CH* 8.1.

46. *SH* 20.4.

47. *CH* 13.13.

48. *CH* 4.11; 12.18.

49. *CH* 10.11.

50. Contrary to *CH* 12.12.

51. *Ascl.* 35.

52. i.e. *logos*, 'reason, speech, discourse'.

53. *CH* 9.1.

54. *CH* 9.10.

55. *CH* 13.13.

56. *SH* 1.2 ; *CH* 7.2.

57. *CH* 10.5.

58. *FH* 12a.

59. *CH* 1.31.

60. *CH* 1.30.

61. *CH* 13.1.

62. *CH* 1.15.

63. *CH* 10.9.

64. *CH* 9.4.

65. *CH* 10.9.

66. *CH* 4.4-5.

67. *CH* 4.3; cf. *CH* 10.25; 12.19, 20; *Ascl.* 6.

68. *CH* 4.2; *Ascl.* 41.

69. *stac'uac* 'possession' (*ktēsis*) can also mean 'creature' (*ktisis*).

Some manuscripts close to F punctuate the text differently, from the end of 5.3 up to the first sentence of 6.1: 'Only man has Nous and speech (6.1), just like the gods. Man (is) a possession of God and the world a possession of man.' This might make sense. But in a wider hermetic context, we can hardly admit that man shares the privilege of *Nous* with the (astral) gods. Indeed we read in *NH* 6.67,12-15 that, unlike man, gods are deprived of *gnôsis* and *epistêmê* (science).

70. Cf. *CH* 10.4.

71. Cf. *CH* 4.9; 13.3.

72. *CH* 1.15; *Ascl.* 7.22; *NH* 6.67,32-4.

73. *CH* 10.13.

74. *CH* 11.20; 13.11.

75. So in Greek. The Armenian reads: 'You will remember nothing of what (belongs) to it', which may be better.

76. So in Greek. The Armenian reads: 'As to those who care for the present (things) the future (ones) follow close upon the present.' This difference is likely due to a misreading of the Greek text (*pronoousi* instead of *proousi*).

77. So in Greek. The Armenian reads: 'the child, once it has gained perfection, goes out of the womb'; *'child'* is sure to be wrong when we compare with the next sentence.

78. *CH* 1.3.

79. Cf. *CH* 10.21.

80. Cf. *CH* 1.22.

81. May be 'if not body and soul'.

82. The 'essential' man of *CH* 1.15 (cf. *Ascl*. 7; *CH* 9.5), i.e. an intelligible essence, which *DH* understands as a 'form' or a 'species'.

83. *eidea = idea*; cf. *DH* 1.1.

84. We reconstruct here the Greek text after *CH* 12.20; see Paramelle-Mahé 1990-91, p. 123 n. 12.

85. *CH* 5.6; 10.4; 14.9; *HHE*, vol. 2, p. 294.

86. Cf. *CH* 1.21; 7.2; *SH* 23.34.

87. *CH* 10.8.

88. *SH* 15.6.

89. *CH* 11.4; 12.13.

90. *krisin*, cf. *CH* 10.11; the Armenian reads *bnutʻiwn* (*phusin*), which may be a corruption of *kʻnnutʻiwn*, nearly equivalent to *krisin*.

91. *CH* 13.3.

92. Cf. *CH* 9.9; *SH* 26.13.

93. *CH* 14.7.

94. *CH* 8.5.

95. *CH* 10.8,9.

96. Perhaps a gloss of the Armenian translator. In medieval Armenian manuscripts ✶ normally means 'star' and ♀ 'sinner'. (For the idea that sins are provoked by astral demons, see *CH* 16.15-16; 9.3; *SH* 6.11.)

97. *CH* 12.7; *SH* 1.1; 7.2.

98. Or according to some manuscripts: 'Every being in this (world) has a nature'.

99. *HO* 2.1.

100. *SH* 4.19; *CH* 9.8.

101. Armenian *anjin* might also mean 'for himself'.

102. *Ascl*. 37; *NH* 6.69,29-32.

103. Cf. *SH* 23.53-62.

104. So in Greek. Armenian 'decreases', which is identical to *SH* 11.2,23.

105. *CH* 10.23.

106. *CH* 10.24.

107. Armenian *aržanawor* should be corrected into *astuacawor* in accordance with Greek *theios*.

108. *CH* 10.23.

109. *CH* 12.2.

110. *CH* 17.

111. ibid.; *SH* 2A.1-2, 15.

112. *CH* 7.2; cf. *CH* 10.21.

113. *CH* 1.27; cf. *SH* 1.29.

114. *CH* 4.2.

115. *Ascl*.12 (*aliis forsitan videtur deridendum*).

116. *CH* 11.20.

117. *CH* 4.3; cf. *CH* 5.2; 16.5; *SH* 6.1.

118. *CH* 5.9; 12.8; 16.3. *Ascl*.1.2, etc.

119. *SH* 18.3.

120. *SH* 11.2,30.

121. *Ascl*. 6.

122. *CH* 11.20.

123. *CH* 4.2.

124. *CH* 10.22.

125. Cf. *CH* 5.9 and Paramelle-Mahé 1990-91, p.127 n.16 for the reconstruction of this difficult passage.

126. *HO* 5.12.

127. *SH* 11.2, 7.

128. *Ascl*.10.

129. *SH* 1.2; *CH* 7.2; 10.5.

130. Cf. *DH* 6.1.

131. *CH* 1.17.

132. *CH* 12.3.

133. *CH* 11.21.

134. *CH* 10.8.

135. *SH* 4.22.

136. *CH* 12.3; cf. *NH* 6.67,10-12.

137. Or 'the whole'; cf. *CH* 1.18.

138. *CH* 4.6; *Ascl*.12.

139. *CH* 4.3.

140. *CH* 10.9.

141. *CH* 12.19.

142. *FH* 21.

143. *NH* 6.68,6-12; *Ascl*. 22.

144. *Ascl*. 6.

145. *Ascl*. 8; cf. *CH* 3.3-4.

146. *SH* 6.12.

147. Cf. *CH* 10.25 for this reconstruction, and *DH* 7.1.

148. *CH* 6.5.

149. *SH* 2A.9.

150. *CH* 4.9.

151. Maybe 'corruption'; cf. *SH* 2A.16.

152. *CH* 11.16; *SH* 26.4; cf. *Ascl.* 19-35 on God Pantomorphos.

153. *SH* 4.6.

154. *SH* 15.1.

155. *CH* 1.20.

156. Cf. *SH* 2A.1; 26.26-7.

157. *CH* 12.2.

158. *CH* 4.3; *Ascl.* 7; cf. *DH* 8.4.

159. *SH* 6.3.

160. *Ascl.* 30; cf. *CH* 11.2.

161. Cf. *SH* 11.2, 42.

162. Cf. *SH* 11.2, 38.

163. *CH* 6.3.

164. *CH* 6.4.

165. *gerašxarhik* = *huperkosmios*.

166. Reasonable, unreasonable and sensible (cf. *HO* 1, 4).

167. May be 'three dimensions', cf. *CH* 13.13.

168. *bnut'iwn* (*phusis*) means here 'generation' (not 'nature').

169. *CH* 12.14; cf. *SH* 12, 13, 14.

170. *SH* 14.1.

171. *DH* 3.2; *CH* 9.3 and *DH* 8.6.

172. *NH* 6.76,4-6; *Ascl.* 27; cf. *SH* 11.2,35; *CH* 8.1.

173. Cf. *DH* 8.6-7.

174. *DH* 10.7 is an addition identical to *SH* 19.1, which we translate here from the Greek as reconstructed in *HHE*, vol. 2, p. 329.

175. *epispatai* (not *epistatai* as in the model of the Armenian version, *gitē*).

176. *CH* 1.14.

177. The text is incomplete. Then follows, in some Armenian manuscripts, an addition drawn from Nemesius ch. 5 (*DH* 11.1-6; cf. *HHE*, vol. 2, pp. 331-2, 402-5).

Bibliography and Abbreviations

Asci. = *Asciepius* (Latin adaptation of DP) in NF vol. 2 and *HHE* vol. 2

Berthelot, M. and Ruelle, E., *Les alchimistes grecs*, vols. 1–3 (Paris s.d.)

Camplani, A., 'Riferimenti biblici nella litteratura ermetica', Annali di storia deli' esegesi 10/2, 1993, 375–425

CH = *Corpus Hermeticum* 1–14 and 16–17 in this edition. *CH* 15 does not exist

Copenhaver, B. P., Hermetica (Cambridge 1992)

De Durand, G.-M., 'Un traité hermetique conserve en arménien', Revue de l'Histoire des Religions 190, 1976, pp. 55–72

DH = *Definitions d'Hermès Trismegiste a Asclépius* (in Armenian translation) in *HHE* vol. 2, and J. Paramelle and J.-P. Mahé, 1991B, *Revuedes Etudes Arméniennes* 22 (1990–91), pp. 115–34, for the Greek fragments

Dorrie, H., 'Der Bote aus dem Matenadaran Bd 3', Gnomon 29, 1957, 445–50

FH = *Fragmenta Hermetica*: *FH* 1036 in NF vol. 4

Fowden, G., The Egyptian Hermes (Cambridge 1986)

Hadot, P., Exercices spirituels et philosophie antique (Paris 1981)

HHE = J.-P. Mahé, *Hermes en Haute-Egypte*, 2 vols. (Quebec,1978; 1982)

HO = *Hermetica Oxoniensia* 1–4: J. Paramelle and J.-P. Mahé, 1991 *Revue des Etudes Grecques*, 104 (1991), pp. 109–39

Ideler, J. L., Physici et medici graeci minores, vol. 1 (Berlin 1841)

Mahé, J.-P. 'Les Definitions d'Hermès Trismégiste a Asclepius', Revue des Sciences Reiigieuses 50, 1976, 193–214

Mahé, J.-P. 'La voie d'immortalité a la lumière des Hermetica de Nag Hammadi et de découvertes plus récentes', Vigiliae Christianae 45, 1991, pp. 347–75

Mahé, J.-P., 'Preliminary remarks on the Demotic Book of Thoth and the Greek Hermetica', Vigiliae Christianae 50, 1996, 353–63

Manandyan, H. and Arevatyan, S., 'Hermeay Eiiameci aü Askiepios sahman' (Definitions of Hermes Trismegistus to Asciepius), Banber Matenadarani 3, 1956, 287–314

NH 1–13 = Coptic codices of Nag Hammadi, containing the following hermetic writings: *NH* 6 (pp. 52, 1–63, 32), *L'Ogdoade et l'Ennéade* (*HHE* vol. 1); *NH* 6 (pp. 63, 33–65, 7), *Prière d'action de graces* (*HHE* 1.1); *NH* 6 (pp. 65, 14–78, 43), *Fragment du Logos Téleios* (*HHE* vol. 2) and other writings more or less influenced by hermetism (the titles in italics do not occur in the codex)

Paramelle, J. and Mahé, J.-P., 'Nouveaux parallèles grecs aux Definitions hermetiques arméniennes', Revue des Etudes Arméniennes 22, 1990–91,115–34

Paramelle, J. and Mahé, J.-P., 'Extraits hermetiques inédits dans un manuscrit d'Oxford', Revue des Etudes Grecques 104, 1991, 109–39

Quispel, G., 'The Gospel of Thomas Revisited', in B. Barc (ed.), Colloque international sur les textes de Nag Hcunmadi (Québec 22–25 août 1978), (Québec 1981) 218–66

SH = *Stobaei Hermetica: SH* 1–22 in NF vol. 3; *SH* 23–9 in NF vol. 4

Terian, A., 'The Hellenizing school, its time, place and scope of activities reconsidered', in N. Garsolan et al. (eds.), East of Byzantium: Syria and Armenia in the Formative Period (Washington 1982), 175–16

Thomson, R. W., Elishe (Eli), History of Vardan and the Armenian War, translation and commentary (Cambridge MA 1982)

BOOKS OF RELATED INTEREST

The Hermetic Tradition
Symbols and Teachings of the Royal Art
by Julius Evola

The Hermetic Science of Transformation
The Initiatic Path of Natural and Divine Magic
by Giuliano Kremmerz

The Lost Pillars of Enoch
When Science and Religion Were One
by Tobias Churton

The Golden Number
Pythagorean Rites and Rhythms in the Development of
Western Civilization
by Prince Matila Costiesco Ghyka
Introduction by Paul Valéry

Awakening Higher Consciousness
Guidance from Ancient Egypt and Sumer
by Lloyd M. Dickie and Paul R. Boudreau

Esoteric Egypt
The Sacred Science of the Land of Khem
by J. S. Gordon

Introduction to Magic
Rituals and Practical Techniques for the Magus
by Julius Evola and the UR Group

Hermetic Herbalism
The Art of Extracting Spagyric Essences
by Jean Mavéric

Inner Traditions • Bear & Company
P.O. Box 388
Rochester, VT 05767
1-800-246-8648
www.InnerTraditions.com

Or contact your local bookseller